DISRUPTER

DISRUPTER

How Maryville University
Remade Itself and
Higher Education

MARTY PARKES

Published by Advantage, Charleston, South Carolina.
Member of Advantage Media Group.

ADVANTAGE is a registered trademark, and the Advantage colophon is a trademark of Advantage Media Group, Inc.

Printed in the United States of America.

10 9 8 7 6 5 4 3 2 1

ISBN: 978-1-64225-283-5
LCCN: 2021910732

Cover design by Fred Cisneros of Cisneros Design.
Layout design by George Stevens.

This publication is designed to provide accurate and authoritative information in regard to the subject matter covered. It is sold with the understanding that the publisher is not engaged in rendering legal, accounting, or other professional services. If legal advice or other expert assistance is required, the services of a competent professional person should be sought.

Advantage Media Group is proud to be a part of the Tree Neutral® program. Tree Neutral offsets the number of trees consumed in the production and printing of this book by taking proactive steps such as planting trees in direct proportion to the number of trees used to print books. To learn more about Tree Neutral, please visit **www.treeneutral.com**.

Advantage Media Group is a publisher of business, self-improvement, and professional development books and online learning. We help entrepreneurs, business leaders, and professionals share their Stories, Passion, and Knowledge to help others Learn & Grow. Do you have a manuscript or book idea that you would like us to consider for publishing? Please visit **advantagefamily.com** or call **1.866.775.1696**.

*To my wife, Catherine, who is worthy of eternal gratitude—
and our two best products who have consumed many
of our dollars in the classroom: daughter Nicole Theron
Parkes, PsyD, and son Trevor Nelson Parkes, Esquire.*

CONTENTS

ACKNOWLEDGMENTS

There's a fallacy about book authorship. Covers normally list only one or two individuals. In reality, I have found it a more crowded situation.

You see, there are actually many people who contribute to the composition of a book. I must start by thanking the trustees, faculty, staff, and alums from Maryville who earned my appreciation through their cooperation and expertise.

Jerry Brisson, a retired Maryville staff member, now lives the good life in Florida. In between rays of sunshine, Jerry served as cheerleader for this project and dutifully reviewed every word.

Mike Bruckner, steadfast friend and retired vice president of public relations at Muhlenberg College in Allentown, Pennsylvania, read the entire manuscript. He challenged some assumptions, which led to a more balanced final product.

Bob Massa, who knows higher education like few others, has mentored me while never losing hope or enthusiasm.

I tip my cap toward Stephen Larkin, Alison Morse, Y-Danair Niehrah, and Alec Stubing of Advantage Books. I especially need to salute Suzanna de Boer, who worked on behalf of Advantage to help me hone the manuscript.

I must single out Maria-Louisa Knierim and Jessica Norris of Maryville's president's office for their great assistance. I likewise praise their predecessors, Jan Johnston and Kathy Lunan, who provided the same helping hand before their well-deserved retirements from the university.

I stand alone on an island regarding any mistakes that may have crept into these pages. Any accolades are gladly shared.

Summer, 2021
Williamsburg, VA

PREFACE

How did this book evolve, and how did I become the chronicler of the Maryville journey? It all began one afternoon. I had always worked in communications, but mostly in sports. The president of Maryville University, Mark Lombardi, was someone I had known all my life, and he had just read in *Sports Illustrated* that I was moving on.

When he called me, he asked, "So what are you going to do?"

And I replied, "Well, to tell you the truth, I love working in communications, but I'd like to try a different industry."

And he said, "How'd you like to come work here at Maryville?" He wanted a fresh perspective on higher education and the university itself. And my surprise turned to a realization over time that my skills would be very applicable in higher education. So I accepted.

From 2009 to 2011, I worked full-time on the Maryville staff heading up the communications department. We did some innovative things during my tenure there that I was proud of. But I was also telecommuting from my home and family in the East. Later, I reluctantly left Maryville to move on to two other schools, heading up communications closer to my home and family in the East. Yet I always stayed in close contact with Maryville and continued to follow and admire its trajectory.

Maryville University has never sat back on its laurels and, under the leadership of Dr. Lombardi, has embarked on a relentless pursuit of excellence and innovation that continues to move the university forward in exceptional and cutting-edge ways. The time came to write a book about Maryville's past along with the strategic ways it has moved forward and continues to progress into the future. Mark asked me to bring my insight to writing a comprehensive book that would be an inspiration as well as a guideline for any institution of higher learning that wanted to find success following Maryville's mindset and example.

The purpose of this book is a profound one. This story can change the future of any university that is struggling now and needs to find a way forward.

I am the author who will tell you the story of Maryville, the disrupter. And I look forward to sharing all that I know about one of the most exciting stories in the history of higher education!

INTRODUCTION

CORONAVIRUS, MARYVILLE, AND HIGHER EDUCATION

The dogmas of the quiet past are inadequate to the stormy present ... As our case is new, so we must think anew, and act anew. We must disenthrall ourselves.

—Abraham Lincoln

The spring 2020 outbreak of the coronavirus in the US—when the original narrative of this book neared completion—has significantly changed US higher education just as it has so many industries and individuals. Every institution has been impacted in some way regardless of size, reputation, or wealth.

This introduction discusses the impacts of the worldwide pandemic on Maryville and higher education. Subsequent sections discuss Maryville's evolution during the last decade to discover how its concerted actions—both deliberate and inadvertent—positioned it well to absorb the punches and resulting body blows delivered by the coronavirus.

The rapid rush by nearly all colleges and universities during 2020 to convert instruction to online platforms to supplement or supplant traditional classroom formats validates virtual courses as a viable, alternative method of instruction. Institutions such as Maryville have led the front of this line by moving away from sole reliance on in-person classrooms and lectures. Such a move appears prophetic in retrospect.

These efforts to blend virtual techniques with, or to supplement, in-person experiences have allowed students to continue to master designated subjects—even when these individuals are not located in the same geographic location as their instructor or counterparts.

Maryville's sustained and forward-looking financial investment in underwriting hard and soft technological costs has also provided proper infrastructure needed to sustain university operations during a time of turmoil and tumult. Connectivity, software, and physical devices like iPads available to all have made such sustainable community activity possible. Many other institutions that did not make such technological investments during the past decade have flagged in contrast. They have found it nearly impossible to function effectively during the coronavirus. These institutions lack the technological tools that permit faculty, students, and staff to communicate and function efficiently while separated physically. Make no mistake: the coronavirus has produced a good deal of angst among the members of the Maryville community. But such stress has been felt much more acutely elsewhere where technological infrastructure lags.

AN ACCELERATION OF A WAVE

When Maryville went completely digital on March 12 of 2020, 87 percent of its traditional students had already taken at least one online course, and many had already taken at least three courses online.

Therefore, Maryville transitioned into a new environment that its students, and to a large extent its faculty and staff, were already somewhat prepared for and familiar with. Now, to be truthful, the university was not prepared to make this transition in a week. But the institution was nonetheless generally prepared to make the transition. And that's what made the difference for Maryville. Its retention numbers held while at the same time its enrollment numbers increased. Maryville entered the fall of 2020 with a 10 percent enrollment bump up, which is a sign of how effectively the institution adapted to the new hurdles. These actions prove the old adage that while you prepare for one thing, you don't realize until afterward that you were really preparing for something else.

Maryville remains largely dependent on tuition revenues from students and/or families to maintain a solid footing. Maintaining robust enrollment and retention levels for domestic and foreign students will, no doubt, prove daunting as the university emerges into a postcoronavirus world. As investment prospectuses constantly warn: past performance is no guarantee of future success.

The president of Maryville, Dr. Mark Lombardi, contends that the coronavirus has actually not changed the trajectory of higher education or the trajectory of its digital future. Instead, it has accelerated that wave by three to five years. He points out that everything that Maryville and others have been doing in recent years to adapt to the new digital age has been accelerated overnight. And now institutions find themselves three to five years further into the future in just a matter of months, not years. That acceleration means higher education is much further down that digital path versus where it thought it would be at this juncture. And that acceleration means many schools are scrambling to adapt and catch up.

"I say the same thing all the time," Lombardi stresses. "This spring, there wasn't a computer file on my laptop that said, 'open this folder in case of pandemic,' with a corresponding list of things to do. Maryville had to create everything from scratch, as so many institutions in higher education and other industries did. But I think I would point out what we call our digital forward strategy during the last several years as the key factor in allowing us to meet these challenges."

Lombardi predicts that a large number of schools are going to end up shutting their doors because they cannot adapt to these profound challenges. A lot of schools simply do not have the resources to considerably upgrade their connectivity and digital outreach. Other institutions struggle with their approach to staff and faculty development in terms of deciding how to teach, how to create learning environments and spaces, and how to design learning techniques that foster student success. These institutions cannot adapt to this postcoronavirus scenario and its hybrid environment of traditional merged with emerging methods.

All of these factors are going to thin the herd of higher education institutions. Maryville's consistent and sustained commitment to technological advancement, along with its continuing investment in faculty and staff development around learning technologies, have proved essential to its success in reacting to the coronavirus challenges. These investments were concentrated in developing very robust and sophisticated learning diagnostics and learning design tools. They paid off through the enhancement of the education the university offers to traditional students as well as creating and supporting a growing and expanding online environment.

MOVING INTO A NEW REALITY

What are some of the specific things that Maryville did? Of course, the university had to perform all the mitigation activities, such as enhanced cleaning and campus maintenance, that other businesses, schools, and industries have had to do. What has also emerged is a complete rethink of buildings, learning spaces, and living spaces design. Maryville certainly has not figured this new environment all out yet. Few, if any individuals, have done so at this point. But this uncertainty has caused Maryville to rethink and reimagine several capital projects that it had on its books. It will sit down with its architects to reconsider some previous design assumptions based on what it has learned during the pandemic about how students are learning in this mixture of digital and on-ground environments—better termed as a hybrid learning environment.

Maryville also had to remake its entire recruitment procedure from an on-ground, in-person, one-on-one experience to a much more virtual one. It utilized countless Zoom calls with prospective parents and students, particularly during the evening hours. Enrollment numbers and participant feedback indicate that this personalized strategy has been quite effective.

Communications strategy, too, has changed dramatically. Its approach has become very much a social media, digital-first approach. This strategy has expanded outreach and connections,

> **Communications strategy, too, has changed dramatically. Its approach has become very much a social media, digital-first approach.**

according to the university. Necessity has bred real invention and real creativity that has borne fruit. For example, applications for next year (autumn 2021) now run about 23 percent ahead of where they were last year at the same time. That's impressive in this turbulent environment, especially when compared with totals from other similar institutions.

Maryville has seen its international student numbers decline because of the pandemic. But there's an interesting sidelight. A number of international students who were unable to enter the United States this fall studied online at Maryville from their home country instead. In other words, the university's digital capabilities and offerings allowed it to retain students from afar despite their inability to come to St. Louis in person because of the pandemic and associated travel restrictions in their home country and/or in the US. Such a trend would not have been possible at other institutions lacking such capabilities, which would have resulted in greater declining enrollment.

Cost considerations have been front and center as well. Maryville has frozen tuition rates for traditional students during the last five years. And beginning this year, it announced the beginning of a lengthy, gradual process to lower tuition for traditional students by 20 percent. It took the first step with a 5 percent reduction this year. The university is well on its way to bending backward the cost curve of higher education. It is able to bend that curve because its budgeting strategy does not simply layer on additional expenses while jacking up charges to students and families. Its approach truly is a very different one than most higher education institutions have engaged in for the last, say, fifty years.

Put another way, the freshmen class and returning class numbers have already been baked into the university's enrollment cake, so to speak. Maryville did not decrease its price tag to increase enrollment. The institution did so because it was the right and smart thing to do to promote student affordability. What impact will it have in next year's enrollment and subsequent years? One guess is as good as another. It will be interesting, for sure, to see.

Lombardi can't say enough about how innovative, adaptive, and committed Maryville's faculty and staff have been, not just during the coronavirus but throughout its long, gradual transition to what he calls "the new university of the twenty-first century." He emphasizes that faculty and staff really are the heroes and the stars of this story. They have learned, developed, and created remarkable learning strategies and techniques. They have adapted to changing conditions, they have learned new skills as the university has gone forward, and they have significantly upped their digital IQs. They have done so much and so much faster than their peers at other learning institutions. Perhaps most important of all, they have served as the pied pipers of Maryville's transition. Such a successful process requires a significant investment of time and energy. This transformation helps these people, for lack of a better term, self-train and self-educate to foster in what many observers call "the digital now revolution."

THE IMPACT ON STUDENTS

What about students? The biggest impact of the pandemic appears to be on the psychological and emotional state of students. A group of young people typically come to college to do two things: to learn and to socially engage with peers. The first part of that equation they can continue to do; the second part is very difficult right now because of circumstances beyond their control. And so, the university remains very concerned about the psychological impact on students. Incidences of counseling services and emotional anxiety have increased greatly as they have throughout society and the wider world. Maryville seeks to provide all the necessary support required in all aspects of student lives. But all that support and commitment to student well-being does not change the simple fact that the current, postpandemic student experience is not what most students really want. Most students, it is felt, realize that the university tries to do everything it can to make it a great experience for students considering the issues facing us today. The university and its students serve as partners in that sense. But students, without any doubt, long for the day where they can receive a vaccine and return to a more normal student life.

How about sports on campus? If organizing a classroom during the coronavirus seems complicated, try organizing competitive athletics. Let us put it this way: it's like trying to solve a Rubik's Cube in the middle of a hurricane in the dark. It is incredibly complicated depending upon the rules and level of physical contact of a given sport. Obviously low-contact sports such as cross country or golf are much easier to pull off, if you will, than basketball or wrestling. As a result, it has been an incredibly difficult time for intercollegiate athletics.

To give you an idea of just how difficult it has been, the Council of Presidents of the Great Lakes Valley Conference, Maryville's National Collegiate Athletic Association (NCAA) Division II conference, has met virtually every two weeks to discuss policies and procedures. Athletic directors have done likewise. Often meetings occur more often than that to discuss emerging issues. Intercollegiate athletics right now remain a very complicated endeavor. Maryville officials are actively engaged in providing the safest environment possible for students so they can enjoy competition and camaraderie. Schools like Maryville do not have the luxury of the National Basketball Association or the National Hockey League, where they can create a multibillion-dollar bubble and place everybody inside it. Certain parts of the NCAA could probably pull that bubble concept off among its Division I Power Five teams, but the rest of NCAA institutions, such as Maryville, are left largely to fend for themselves.

THREE CONCLUSIONS FOR MARYVILLE AND BEYOND

Three key conclusions, then, can be synthesized about the effect the coronavirus has had specifically on Maryville and generally on higher education.

The coronavirus hasn't slowed the future for Maryville specifically and higher education generally. Rather, it's accelerating its pace. Higher education now evolves at a pace more akin to dog years than human ones. The pandemic has not altered the trajectory that higher education has followed in recent years. Rather than changing that path, it has merely accelerated the activity along that arc. The conversion to a flexible, hybrid model of education—underscored by cutting-edge digital tools and infrastructure—has allowed Maryville, despite coronavirus challenges, to continue to react, grow, evolve, and prosper. It has done so in a most novel way. It has actually bent back the cost curve of higher education through implementing a long-term process to decrease its tuition sticker price for traditional students by 20 percent over the next five years. Few other higher education institutions have demonstrated the will and finesse to pull off such a delicate balancing act.

> **"The future exists today, it's just not evenly distributed."**

One of Dr. Lombardi's favorite quotes from William Gibson is "The future exists today, it's just not evenly distributed."[1] These words seem particularly apt during a pandemic. Famous football coach the late George Allen customarily eschewed draft picks and traded them for

---

1 | William Gibson, *Distrust That Particular Flavor* (Penguin UK, 2012).

veteran players. When asked why he seemingly was mortgaging away the future prospects of his team, Allen retorted, "The future is now." Dr. Lombardi's contention, in some ways, buttresses Allen's philosophy. Emerging technological and market forces have altered a staid industry (higher education) in ways almost unimaginable just a short time ago. Modes of instruction, types of facilities, and extracurricular activities have all been rapidly altered in a profound way. Yet, that alteration has not occurred equally across the board in the same way everywhere. Some institutions can bring greater financial resources to bear. Others have carved out market niches that have distinguished them from other institutions. Still others have utilized their geographic location and/or physical campuses to provide congenial, safe environments appealing to parents and prospective students alike. Each institution bears careful observation and evaluation, as the marketplace that is composed of traditional and nontraditional students evaluates opportunity versus cost. Universities such as Maryville that have long and thoughtfully grappled with these emerging implications while adapting to the onslaught of administrative needs brought about by the coronavirus will likely foster degrees of imitation from those institutions fortunate enough to survive.

Maryville University stands as a model of the new university of the twenty-first century. The pace of change in higher education will not abate any time soon. Much of the impact of the coronavirus will eventually dissipate. But that does not mean the higher education industry will be able to return to its old, and some would contend, staid ways. Rather, its underlying tenets will be reevaluated, reexamined, and reconsidered at a rapid clip. A new generation of prospective students, shaped by a digital background where a myriad of alternatives can be compared and contrasted with a few clicks of a keyboard, will prove shrewd customers demanding a customized, affordable experience concentrated on their specific situations and needs. The era of standardized higher education has passed. The new model of the twenty-first century is universities like Maryville focusing in a fully digital, laser-like fashion on its students and their service needs. After all, the future is here and now—and not evenly distributed.

SETTING THE STAGE

Picture a leafy campus of a venerable university located in a fashionable suburb of St. Louis. While such a setting appears tranquil and peaceful on the surface, turmoil lurks beneath. Challenges—internal and external, new and old—require decisive action. The university has come perilously close to death before. Yet somehow it survived. Maryville sets out to demonstrate Nelson Mandela's belief that courage is not the absence of fear but the triumph over it.

TURBULENCE

Colleges and universities—like airplanes—encounter turbulence. And such turbulence has become more frequent and reached greater levels during the past decade or so. Even if we strip away the hyperbolic headlines and exhortations of extremist critics, certain indisputable facts about higher education stand out.

▶ **Tuition levels continue to climb annually at a rate much faster than family incomes.** These higher levels result from soaring institutional costs amid flat or declining enrollments. Never has institutional competition in recruiting students been more intense. Schools add facilities, staff, and programs to try to attract the attention of prospective students and their parents. Yet these targeted students are declining on a national level, and their demographic makeup is skewing to more first-generation prospects and students of diverse backgrounds. Flat or declining enrollments combined with increasing costs means more revenue must be squeezed from existing students and their families to make up for budget shortfalls. Family costs increase inexorably as a result. So does student debt.

▶ **First-generation students, predominantly from low-income and/or minority households, struggle to recognize higher education as a viable path.** It remains difficult for first-generation prospective students to afford and also master the intricacies of the higher education marketplace in order to join it. This segment represents approximately one-quarter of prospective students in a given year. That group will continue to grow throughout the next twenty years.

▶ **Retention and completion rates are less than rosy.** Reputable estimates contend that while 70 percent of the general US population will study at a four-year college or university at some point during their lives, less than two-thirds of this 70 percent will graduate and earn a degree. Thirty percent of college and university students, in fact, drop out after their first year. Sixty percent of college and university dropouts receive no financial help from their families.[2] Of those who persevere and graduate, large numbers require more than four years to complete their degree. Additional semesters spent earning a bachelor's degree typically rack up more student debt than the standard four-year span while requiring a student to forego full-time work and associated earnings.

---

2 | Anthony P. Carnevale, Stephen J. Rose and Ban Cheah, "The College Payoff: Education, Occupations, Lifetime Earnings," The Georgetown University Center on Education and the Workforce, https://cew.georgetown.edu/wp-content/uploads/2014/11/collegepayoff-complete.pdf.

▶ **Institutional leadership is habitually slow to consider and adopt policies that place student needs and learning outcomes at the center of all campus decisions.** Often the priorities, preferences, and convenience of faculty, staff, and alumni dominate such discussions and decisions. Many institutions refrain from offering students an option to attend classes on a year-round basis and complete their degrees in fewer than four years, enabling them to join the workforce more quickly. Schools cling to the notion that a college education should be a four-year experience with summers off. This four-year format may work fine for many students. But for others, a condensed time frame might be preferable if such an option were offered.

▶ **Technology exerts unrelenting pressure to deliver educational experiences in new, innovative, and customized ways.** Sensitivity to the preferences and daily schedules of students— whether traditional, full-time students, or working adults—has increasingly become a crucial factor in successful recruitment and retention. Yet many colleges and universities resist these trends. They remain committed exclusively to traditional academic programs, delivery methods (in-person, in-class faculty lectures), and rigid schedules. Struggles to maintain sufficient enrollment levels often, unsurprisingly, result when customer needs and preferences are ignored or dismissed.

▶ **Many economists, students, and parents increasingly question whether a college education makes financial sense.** These individuals increasingly wonder whether funding a college education represents a good return on their investment (ROI). These questions have become increasingly prevalent during the past decade. Before then, general consensus favored investment in a college education. Why? A college graduate possessing a bachelor's degree typically earns 84 percent more over their lifetime than a high school graduate.[3] Those individuals without a college degree are also twice as likely to be unemployed as those who possess one and subsequently accrue greater personal wealth over their lifetimes. Soaring tuition rates, increasing student debt, high dropout or noncompletion rates, large numbers of students requiring more than four years to complete their degree, and relatively stagnant employee real wages (after inflation) have increasingly called into question whether a college education still represents a worthwhile financial investment.

▶ **Perhaps most disturbing of all, many colleges and universities remain unable or unwilling to provide straightforward, simple examples of positive financial returns on investment enjoyed by their graduates.** These institutions often lack accurate data about the accomplishments of their alumni. They are unable to formulate simple cost-benefit financial analysis that can be used to demonstrate the value of their institution's degree.

ROI—RETURN ON INVESTMENT FOR COLLEGE DEGREE RECIPIENTS

Indeed, the benefits to the students who receive a degree are well-documented. A February 2021 segment on NPR's *All Things Considered* featuring the president of Morehouse College in Atlanta, Dr.

---

3 | Tiffany Hsu, "College Graduates Earn 84% More Than High School Grads, Study Says," *Los Angeles Times*, August 5, 2011, https://latimesblogs.latimes.com/money_co/2011/08/college-Gradutates-pay.html.

David Thomas, referenced that, on average, a college degree recipient earns approximately $1 million more through their career than a person with a high school diploma. Of course, this will vary by geography, major, quality of school and other factors, but the difference remains significant over time.

While it is true that the system in its previous form is broken in a number of respects, the principle and centrality

On average, a college degree recipient earns approximately $1 million more through their career than a person with a high school diploma.

of higher education remains as vital as ever. The need for vibrant and effective higher education in our nation has never been more essential. Its ability to transform society for the better has never been more important. And the digital transformation age of this century is ushering in the creation of myriad new careers that will need educated and qualified practitioners to work in and master those new professions. But like all great entities that provide an essential public good, the university must adapt, evolve, change, and reinvent itself. If it resists or refuses to do so, destruction may result.

That scenario leads us to St. Louis, Missouri, at the time of the onset of the Great Recession (December 2007–June 2009) and a heretofore unknown private university in its suburbs called Maryville University. Why and how did Maryville University craft and implement a strategy to remake many facets of higher education when other institutions were stalled or pulling back in retreat? Why and how did this institution embed bedrock values—such as ambition, accessibility, speed, collaboration, courage, innovation, nimbleness, shrewdness, and vision—within its culture, causing it to act quickly and decisively? Why and how did this university update its delivery of services and forge a new model in personalized learning? Why and how has Maryville created a model for change in higher education that will light a path for its continual reinvention?

This book describes the people, processes, and programs that have brought significant success to Maryville at a time of retrenchment in higher education. This narrative chronicles an inspiring story about how Maryville has prospered and actually thrived in the face of severe challenges. *U.S. News & World Report* has twice named Maryville the No. 1 Over-Performing University in the nation in 2013 and 2014 while *The Chronicle of Higher Education* has recently designated Maryville as the second-fastest growing private university in the nation (2020).[4]

This book is not simply a how-to book for insiders such as college administrators, trustees, faculty, or students. Reading these pages and then attempting to implement Maryville University's exact same steps at another institution will not guarantee success. In fact, such haphazard application of the lessons contained in these pages may result in creating more challenges.

> These traits, and examples of their application, provide a framework for building the new university of the future—a university where no matter what the issue, student learning and outcomes remain paramount and at the center.

This story, rather, is designed to provide a roadmap of a kind for varied readers—including students and their families. It describes the traits of one institution that has navigated many hurdles by reinventing the values and principles on which universities have traditionally been based. These traits, and examples of their application, provide a framework for building the new university of the

4 | "Maryville University Ranked No. 1 Over-Performing University in Nation," Maryville University, https://www.maryville.edu/no-1-over-performing-university-in-nation/.

future—a university where no matter what the issue, student learning and outcomes remain paramount and at the center. What may strike the reader is that the Maryville story is far afield from an institution utilizing a huge endowment or Nobel Prize-winning faculty of national prominence as springboards to success. What this story demonstrates is that it is precisely unheralded institutions like Maryville that possess a commitment toward freedom of action, flexibility of thought, and ultimately the courage to affect change. Many institutions pontificate about the need to affect change but back away when it comes time to act and implement. Maryville, instead, has acted with courage, confidence, and resolve to lead a revolution.

TRANSFORMATION OF HIGHER EDUCATION

One can plausibly contend that higher education has been transformed more in the past decade than in the previous thousand years.

For centuries, a college or university achieved esteem as a physical location within a geographic community. Faculty, mostly white and male, devoted years of serious, solitary study to their disciplines. They lectured to students (predominantly male) seated in rows, facing them in classrooms. These students—whether by economics, religion, gender, and/or social status—represented an elite few culled from the masses. Students earned their place through demonstrating their ability to absorb information in lectures and reflect this mastery during written exams or essays. Little, if any, learning occurred between students. Rather, information flowed predominantly one way—from professor to student. This flow evolved because professors owned the knowledge and content. Institutions enjoyed and benefited from this monopoly of content and/or knowledge within geographic areas. If one wanted an education, attending a nearby physical college or university was frequently a student's only option.

Technology has crushed that monopoly during the twenty-first century. Content and knowledge now belong to any individual with an internet connection. Any person who carries a cell phone has a vast, comprehensive library of information available at their fingertips. They can access more information in a single day than their parents could within their lifetimes. And the pace by which this transformation has occurred is dizzying. This democratization and distribution of content will only accelerate in the months and years ahead as new technological modes supplant what we now classify as cutting edge.

Learning, therefore, now takes place everywhere. Institutions of higher education compete across town, across state lines, across the nation, and, increasingly, around the world for students, faculty, resources, and recognition. A typical student currently focuses less and less on sitting at a particular desk in a particular classroom at a particular time listening to a particular professor lecture to them about a particular subject. Information instead flows constantly in multiple directions and through multiple mechanisms between professors and students. This transmission of information occurs around the clock instead of within designated time frames. Students have the ability to learn as much or sometimes more from other students or from internet resources as they do from the professor.

Instruction is increasingly undertaken in a personalized, customized way rather than in impersonal, one-size-fits-all lectures. Teaching techniques intentionally take into account the personal background, learning preferences, and career goals of students. Learning outcomes focus less on regurgitating information from lectures. Rather, varied methods of evaluation are incorporated through group-based discussions, presentations, and problem-solving projects. In other words, teacher-centered delivery has been supplanted by team-oriented methods that increasingly reflect the needs of the workplace. The arsenal of teaching methods, in summary, has been supplemented and expanded.

Those institutions that can adapt and provide such personalized experiences will thrive. They will demonstrate value and a solid return on their customer's investment. Please note that word "customer" is chosen with intent. When an organization or institution offers a service to someone who pays for it and who has choices concerning how and where to receive that service, they are by definition a customer. And customer aptly describes millions of people who pay higher education tuition bills each year—even if some people who work on college campuses are offended by the application of what has previously been considered a business term to academia.

Competition can sometimes spell institutional doom in the turbulent higher education marketplace. More than ninety nonprofit universities have closed since 2013. Estimates by experts such as the late Clay Christensen of Harvard University predict that one thousand such nonprofit institutions will close by 2022.[5] Yet, Maryville University has actually recognized and embraced the challenges prevalent in higher education. It has acted carefully, quickly, and ably to identify and assess opportunities. It has steadfastly maintained focus on its students and their learning outcomes. Its teaching techniques have remained flexible based on the needs of each learner. It has fostered a constant hunger for steady institutional innovation and progress where new ideas are welcomed and evaluated expeditiously: "act fast, fail fast, learn faster, and succeed." Finally, it has paid attention to sequencing its action steps properly so that the right decisions are made and implemented at the right time by the right people.

---

5 | Max Nisen, "Clay Christensen: Higher Education Is 'On the Edge of the Crevasse'," Yahoo Finance, February 12, 2013, https://finance.yahoo.com/news/clay-christensen-higher-education-edge-012403255.html.

EVOLUTION OF THE UNIVERSITY

Maryville University, like St. Louis, owes much of its heritage to the influence of the French. Maryville's founders were members of the Society of the Sacred Heart, a religious order from France. Sacred Heart nuns acquired in 1862 a 21-acre parcel known as Withnell's Grove in south St. Louis and established a school for women that evolved through the years. In January of 1921, Maryville received full accreditation by the State of Missouri as a junior college. Maryville became a full four-year college in 1923.

By 1957, the 21-acre campus parcel in south St. Louis had become cramped. The nuns acquired 290 acres of land in what was then rural West County between Route 40 and Conway Road. It was a gutsy move to leave their then-metropolitan location in the late 1950s for the woods of West County. Chalk this decision up as an early indication of the institution's innovation and resilience.

The new West County campus was formally dedicated on April 23, 1961. The initial transition went rather smoothly. But the 1960s eventually proved problematic. Financial and other challenges confronted small colleges for women such as Maryville. Many such institutions closed while others consolidated with men's schools or opted to join a state educational system underwritten by taxpayers. Maryville chose an alternate path. It announced in 1968 that it would accept male students. Three men registered in 1969.

Coeducation, however, did not cure all ills. Finances remained precarious. Circumstances again required innovation and resilience as Maryville celebrated its centennial year in 1972, when a lay board of trustees assumed ownership from the Society of the Sacred Heart. Confidential plans were formulated for an announcement of closure if circumstances could not be improved. Just at this moment of need and opportunity, nearby Mercy Hospital (then known as St. John's) contributed an outright grant of badly needed funds to help keep Maryville afloat in return for incorporating Mercy's nursing school and introducing other health programs.

This alliance with Mercy saved the institution and transformed its prospects for the future. Innovative health programs attracted more students as enrollment reached 1,200. Budgets were balanced. Institutional reinvestment took many forms, including the purchase of another 150 acres adjacent to campus. It is important to note that throughout its history and despite daunting obstacles, academics remained rigorous in the tradition established by the Society of the Sacred Heart. The lay board decided to hire its first nonreligious and male leader, Dr. Claudius Pritchard, in 1977. Dr. Pritchard took another bold, innovative step. He recognized the growing need—long before others did—for the education of working adults in the St. Louis region. Thus, Maryville's Weekend & Evening College launched in the spring semester of 1981. The W&E College boosted Maryville's scope, reach, and reputation among both traditional and new audiences. Enrollment climbed and enhanced the institution's financial standing through diversification of its revenue streams through the introduction of a new audience of students.

The following year, on June 1, the official name of the institution changed from Maryville College to Maryville University to reflect its expansion. Dr. Keith Lovin succeeded Pritchard as Maryville's president in 1992. The pattern of positive developments accelerated during his successful tenure at the helm, including Maryville's celebration of its 125-year anniversary in 1997. A $26.5 million Building for Leadership fundraising campaign concluded in 2003. New facilities and programs sprang up. Maryville had become a much stronger institution under Lovin, and it now initiated a search for his successor.

Dr. Mark Lombardi received appointment as the next president of Maryville University in the spring of 2007. On the surface, it appeared he had trod a traditional path to a college presidency. He had earned bachelors and doctoral degrees in political science at two Big Ten universities before spending the next quarter century in the classroom earning tenure as a full professor. Ultimately, though, Lombardi shifted to the administrative side of academia. There, his experiences convinced him that campus constituencies—whether at various public and private institutions in the Midwest, South, and Southwest where he had served—often devote more passion, thought, and effort to resisting the forces of change rather than embracing them.

Lombardi came to appreciate Maryville's traditional and demonstrable proclivity for academic rigor, reinvention, and resilience during his interview process. Such traits, he concluded, would provide an ideal institutional foundation for constructing a new breed of university. Here, he felt he could instill a new matrix of values rooted in speed, flexibility, and innovation buttressed by fiscal prudence and blue-sky experimentation. Lombardi surmised that such a battle-tested institution could flourish in the midst of a multitude of disruptive forces. For all these reasons, Lombardi believed he had landed in the right place with the right characteristics at the right time when he assumed his presidential duties on June 15, 2007. He could see that Maryville University was poised and ready to navigate and reconfigure the increasingly turbulent higher education landscape.

PHASE I

GROWTH AND VISION AMID TURMOIL

Some of Maryville University's achievements have stemmed from an incessant restlessness. Another part of its success comes from possessing the vision to recognize emerging opportunities on, or sometimes just beyond, the horizon. Yet another part results from having the financial acumen to invest in the right opportunities while sequencing action steps properly. The university encourages risk-taking and remains unafraid to act quickly and decisively.

THE ENROLLMENT FACTOR

Enrollment is the lifeblood of nearly all colleges and universities. Except for a select number with huge endowments, the future of thousands of institutions hinges largely on their ability to attract a sufficient number of new students while retaining enough existing ones each semester.

Most college students and their families must be able to pay tuition, fees, and, where applicable, room and board. Their payments—normally subsidized by financial aid advanced by institutions themselves, generous scholarship donors, and federal student loans—collectively represent the lion's share (usually three-quarters or more) of institutional income for most schools. Most remaining institutional income results from philanthropic support given by alumni, staff, faculty, and donors (including corporate ones). Some schools also derive grant income from national, state, and local governmental entities. But the bottom line is that most institutions stay afloat predominantly through payments by students and their families.

This situation translates into incessant pressure on institutions to recruit a sufficient number of academically qualified students from families who can afford to defray some or much of the cost of their student's college education. Layered upon this reality is the desire of most institutions to ensure a diverse student population from varying geographic locations, race and ethnic backgrounds, and economic standings. Such desired diversity usually requires substantial financial support in the way of scholarships and subsidies to underwrite deserving students. Finding this right mix is seldom easy or inexpensive.

These factors cause sleepless nights among enrollment professionals. Many campus constituencies find the quantifiable nature of enrollment—number of applicants, ethnic composition of the student body, number of campus visits, number of enrolled students, and number of applicants versus number of enrollees, known as the yield rate—to be a convenient way to render judgment regarding the effectiveness of an enrollment division. Such simplistic measurements tend to lessen job security and promote relatively high turnover within the profession itself. Much like athletic coaches, enrollment professionals remain only as good as last season's performance. This situation encourages short-term expediency rather than long-term focus. These factors underlie why *The Chronicle of Higher Education* has published articles with titles such as "The Hottest Seat on Campus" to describe the daunting task facing enrollment professionals.

Demographic trends have made the task even more difficult. The baby boom generation has passed. The number of potential college students graduating currently from high schools has dwindled. This trend is most pronounced in the Northeastern and Midwestern states. Colleges and universities increasingly contend for a smaller number of full-time, traditional undergraduate students. At the same time, rising tuition and other costs have raised the price tag for families during a time when family incomes have remained relatively stagnant. Affordability suffers, application numbers drop, and campus visits fall. That combination strikes at the heart of the ability of many higher education institutions to survive and thrive.

This scenario explains why so many colleges and universities have targeted international students to supplement domestic ones. It also helps explain why many institutions have also developed online, graduate, and part-time programs. Such programs entice nontraditional student enrollment to bolster declining populations of traditional, full-time undergraduates. Some observers describe the state of competition today for traditional, full-time students as cutthroat. Many institutions barely survive from one year to the next. *The Wall Street Journal* routinely publishes stories entitled "Liberal Arts Colleges, in Fight for Survival, Focus on Job Skills" to highlight such fierce competition.

Maryville University does not evaluate the success of its enrollment division simply by measuring how many applicants it rejects, known as "selectivity" in the trade, or how high it is ranked by annual college rating services. Rather it focuses on providing broad access and opportunity by admitting large numbers of committed, qualified students who demonstrate they will benefit from Maryville's rigorous programs of study. Bottom line: **The institution judges its success**

by how much opportunity it creates rather than by how much access it restricts.

Total enrollment comprising all undergraduate, graduate, and online students has climbed to more than 11,000 from all US states and more than fifty-five countries. Traditional full-time undergraduates number nearly 3,000, with more than 8,000 in graduate and undergraduate programs for working adults including more than 5,300 online. In contrast, in 2007, these numbers stood at 3,300 in total with roughly 1,600 traditional and 1,700 working adults with none online. Amid this growth, graduation rates have increased from 63 percent to 75 percent. Perhaps most telling of all, these degree recipients enjoy a 98 percent career placement rate after graduation. That is a true success story that clearly shows the value and ROI of attending the university.

After attending Maryville, 98 percent of students are employed within their chosen field or enrolled in graduate school within six months of graduation.

The university continues to enjoy a period of expansive enrollment. Its original enrollment goal of 10,000 students by 2022 has been recalibrated to 25,000 by 2025. What has become clear is that Maryville does not rely exclusively on one generational segment nor one constituency of society to meet its enrollment goals. Instead, it simultaneously engages several geographic markets, population segments, and academic programs to reach its enrollment goals.

Analysis reveals two main factors underlying why Maryville has generated robust enrollment figures at a time when other institutions have retrenched: this is due to high-quality academic programs that are designed to generate positive student outcomes along with the utilization of technology, informed by data analytics, in driving enrollment decisions.

CRAFTING A DYNAMIC ENROLLMENT STRATEGY

Jeffery D. Miller joined the Maryville staff as vice president of enrollment not long after Mark Lombardi assumed its presidency. Throughout the next decade, Miller and his colleague Shani Lenore joined forces in plotting a strategy and using technology to recruit greater numbers of students across the national and international landscape. Such a long-term, harmonious partnership between two skilled enrollment professionals at one institution is unusual in higher education. And it paid dividends.

One strategic decision that proved essential was to break out the adult and online recruitment efforts into a complementary new division named Adult & Online Education. The creation of this specialized unit sharpened focus on the adult online marketplace for both undergraduate and graduate programs. A centralized Enrollment Operations Center, meanwhile, tied the Enrollment Division for traditional undergraduates and the School of Adult & Online Education together and ensured some degree of continuity and coordination.

THE IMPACT OF GEODEMOGRAPHIC RESEARCH

Lenore emphasizes the utilization of technology and data in Maryville's enrollment activities. She recalls that the university introduced the use of geodemographic research to identify students who lived in households in communities that typically mirrored the behavior of the households of students who matriculated from Maryville and demonstrated success. Geodemographic market research has since become standard in much of higher education. But when Miller and Lenore teamed up, its use was not yet widespread. As its name implies, this strategy ties geography and demographics together. It is a concept that corporations have utilized for years. It largely explains how businesses target households. Through analysis of customer habits and household demographics, corporations seek out behavioral and demographic characteristics that reveal the right individuals to target.

Such research provided Maryville criteria to target zip codes featuring 50 percent or more of student households possessing demographic and lifestyle characteristics of students who had proved a good fit previously. For example, Maryville could target a nontraditional recruiting area in southern California and know precisely which zip codes to zero in on with a high probability of success. Academic information about these students culled from existing educational sources was then combined with this geodemographic analysis of households. Their intersection proved the sweet spot that generated significant enrollment growth.

Of course, Maryville could not feasibly recruit every student from every zip code who indicated good potential. Where to start then? A couple of tactics require specific mention. First, Maryville made an institutional decision to move up to NCAA Division II athletics and join the Great Lakes Conference. This conference, arguably the premier one in Division II, required Maryville's athletic teams to compete in communities throughout the Midwest from Kansas City to Chicago, Indianapolis, and Louisville. The enrollment division decided to target its outreach in zip codes in Great Lakes Conference communities where its geodemographic analysis indicated promise.

The other decision was to concentrate efforts simultaneously in select states in other areas of the country that featured a growing population of college-aged students. The key states that Maryville targeted were California and Texas. The university deployed full-time, territory-based recruiters in those states. These recruiters served as a local sales force supported by the home office in St. Louis. As a bonus, California and Texas tended to offer a more diverse student population than Midwestern states. Recruitment of such a rich diversity of students satisfied dual goals of more ethnic diversity from varied geographic locations.

Success in California and Texas demonstrates that Maryville's enrollment programs have permeated due to its precise, targeted approach. Members of the enrollment division staff do not currently travel to all fifty states. But Maryville now receives applications from all fifty states. These numbers reflect the best of both worlds: Maryville's reach in its traditional markets remains quite strong while the percentage of Midwestern students has dwindled a bit as a component of the overall percentage of its student population.

Digital marketing underscores Maryville's recruitment system. It has helped the university decide where to travel efficiently and which students they should target during high school visits and college fairs. When asked what distinguishes Maryville's recruiting approach compared with other institutions, Miller and Lenore

Digital marketing underscores Maryville's recruitment system.

both point to the university's consistent and sophisticated use of technology and data within its digital marketing. Maryville does not waste time recruiting in areas with a low probability of success. Miller admits it is sometimes tough to utilize technology to analyze data—while ignoring a highly touted college fair or high school visit—and stay disciplined within its approach. But Maryville's geodemographic research process has proved highly successful in determining the best locations with the highest success rates. So Maryville's focus remains there.

ADDITIONAL FACTORS FOR SUCCESS

Several other factors also have contributed to Maryville's enrollment success: the construction of pipelines; increasing emphasis on global programming and international students; rising full-time residential populations on campus; an improved campus-visit experience; enhanced communications outreach leveraging digital connectivity and integrated use of print, web, and social media; continual highlighting of the success of Maryville graduates; and a personalized process for handling the nuts and bolts of application submission, review, and notification.

Being market focused and creating new academic programs and extracurricular activities that appeal to prospective students has remained a hallmark of the approach. For example, Maryville determined that cybersecurity was a dynamic new field. Many high school students had become intrigued by the possibility of a career in the field. Yet few academic institutions offer such a four-year degree. Maryville moved quickly in three months to secure proper staff, computer capabilities, classroom facilities, and academic oversight. This new program has provided a pipeline of students who come to Maryville specifically to enroll in that program.

On the extracurricular front, cheer and dance programs were added several years ago. Now fifty to sixty students participate annually in them. Adding varsity sports such as wrestling, lacrosse, and ice hockey have created new pipelines. It is highly unlikely that many of these students would have enrolled at Maryville without the availability of such extracurricular options. Combine these types of initiatives with the introduction of online academic programs, and you witness an expansion and explosion in overall enrollment levels.

Maryville has also expanded the university's study abroad and international recruitment opportunities. In 2007, there were a total of seven international students; Maryville boasted more than three hundred in 2019. In 2007, the university sent a handful of students on study abroad; in 2019, more than 180 study overseas.

Maryville has simultaneously sought to increase its residential population. In 2019, that number stands at nearly 1,100 compared to 500 in 2007 with significantly upgraded quality of student housing. Hand in hand with the enhanced residence halls came a plethora of new facilities including a dining hall, a Starbucks in the library, revitalized learning spaces with state-of-the-art technology, and a student life building designed for student engagement and collaboration.

SELLING AN INTANGIBLE PRODUCT

Miller recalls that early in his career, he realized that marketing a college education is tantamount to selling an intangible product. Thus, an effective campus-visit program was crucial since it ranks among the most tangible aspects of a university's product offerings. After arriving in St. Louis, Miller engaged a consultant who specialized in campus-visit experiences to review Maryville's procedures. He shared their findings widely on campus. Signage has been increased and, in some cases, relocated to provide better visibility. Consistent branding and use of colors, imagery, and a new logo have been introduced. Meeting spaces have been upgraded and reconfigured. Group presentations by college officials from outside the enrollment office have been added. Campus tours, although still conducted by student guides, have been revamped to allow visitors to see campus features such as Walker Hall's digital wall or touch the bell from the original south St. Louis campus located on the main quadrangle. All these factors, Miller believes, have made the Maryville experience seem more tangible to prospective students and their families. He notes with pride that, according to the visit consultant, Maryville was the only university in his experience that implemented every recommendation made.

OUTREACH

Enhanced communications outreach to prospective students and their parents is another area to which Maryville has devoted much focus. While some rather muted outreach may occur earlier than the sophomore year, more aggressive targeting commences at that point. Maryville then begins to purchase names and addresses of prospective students who fit the right academic profile and are located within zip codes that the geodemographic research has identified as likely to yield new students. Many of these students and their families have no previous familiarity with Maryville at all. Developing brand awareness becomes a first step.

Outreach relies on several tools, including elements of digital, print, and social media. Maryville gets the ball rolling by utilizing Internet Protocol (IP) targeting in online campaigns. Some have described IP targeting as akin to traditional, print direct mail campaigns delivered through electronic means. The process is as follows: Maryville takes a physical household address and runs it through a computer system so an IP address can be identified and matched. Then the university starts running pertinent online ads to that household. Anybody in that household—student and parent alike—may receive an online ad from Maryville. This process is repeated continually throughout their search via this internet tool.

The university supplements this initial outreach with targeted email campaigns as well as retargeting techniques based on a student's online behavior. If a student opens an email from Maryville or visits certain pages on the Maryville website, they will be retargeted and sent follow-up information electronically. The university employs "geo-fencing," which is the ability to identify a particular geographic location, high school, or event such as a college fair and send ads to individuals through their mobile devices.

Maryville does not consider print materials obsolete. It has scaled back its use of print but not abandoned it. The university feels that many parents still read print pieces and are likely to share select elements with their student. Households receiving print pieces have hopefully developed at least some familiarity with Maryville electronically by the time the print pieces arrive in their mailbox.

Maryville believes the university's website working in tandem with a vibrant social media outreach is its most powerful and important marketing tool. Therefore, the university maintains a mindset that there is no such thing as "done" where its website is concerned. Continuous production of content and enhancement remains a given. Content seldom becomes static or stale. Toward this end, Maryville has hired staff who remain committed to continual production of video and other multimedia. This dynamic information is available and responsive across all platforms and devices. It conveniently reaches students, who spend much of their day looking at mobile devices, wherever they happen to be.

Social media has proved an important aspect of enrollment outreach as well. The university maintains a vibrant presence on Facebook, Twitter, Instagram, and other platforms. Words and pictures are integrated to convince the audience that Maryville is a place awash with interesting events and personal accomplishment. Facebook ad campaigns are utilized on occasion. Campus community members, including faculty, reach out on a regular basis to post comments or engage with prospective students and their families.

The university maintains constant emphasis on the career accomplishments of its alumni—particularly its recent graduates. These testimonials underscore that Maryville graduates do not just receive jobs but secure rewarding careers. The university expends substantial effort to stay in close touch with its alumni and track their progress. In recent years, 98 percent of all students had secured professional employment or were pursuing graduate study within months of commencement. Thus, statistics indicate that the overwhelming majority of Maryville alumni encounter rapid success in the job market or their graduate studies. That is why Maryville has consistently been ranked in the top 15 percent of return on investment based on the Educate to Careers ranking.

A PERSONALIZED PROCESS

The final aspect of Maryville's enrollment procedures underscores the personalization of the process. Maryville does not evaluate the success of its enrollment campaigns based on how many students it rejects or how exclusive its accepted class appears statistically. In the words of Trustee Chris Chadwick, "We are not interested in separating wheat from chaff; we want everybody to succeed." The university has formulated an evaluative structure where each applicant comes to know an individual admission counselor. Great care is exercised to ensure that accepted students should thrive at Maryville. Thus, the university's personalized

Great care is exercised to ensure that accepted students should thrive at Maryville.

enrollment process meshes well with its philosophy of individualized education.

What are some specific steps that Maryville has put in place? A holistic evaluative approach is taken with all applicants. No one factor determines acceptance or rejection. That philosophy partly explains why Maryville made submission of standardized test results optional a few years ago. Since the enrollment process is based on a belief that fit at the institution is the most important factor, the university does not wish to dismiss applicants purely on the basis of a standardized test score.

Once a decision has been communicated to a candidate, Maryville initiates a process to convince each student to accept its invitation to enroll. Personalized messages are sent electronically by email or social media from students, faculty, and administrators. Some of this outreach is less formal but fun. For example, one acceptance pool received a Lego kit to construct the Maryville logo. Once a deposit is received, Maryville sends each individual a Maryville Saints flag they can fly in their yard or in their room to demonstrate school spirit and pride. This process continues throughout the summer until classes start in the fall to guard against "summer melt."

In summary, all the factors outlined have allowed Maryville's enrollment programs to flourish. Miller became vice president of strategic trends in March of 2018 with Lenore replacing him as vice president of enrollment. This process demonstrates the long-term continuity underscoring enrollment success.

NO MARGIN, NO MISSION

Those words were repeatedly uttered for many years by Maryville's now retired Chief Financial Officer (CFO) Larry Hays. They underline the importance of generating annual surpluses to fund continual rein-vestment. This phrase has taken on added significance during the past decade when Maryville's rapid pace of innovation and expansion has required ongoing funding. Maryville's ability to execute sound financial discipline and shrewd budgeting has generated substantial annual surpluses.

There is another phrase that current Chief Financial Officer Steve Mandeville uses to describe Maryville's financial success: "Not for profit is not a business model!" It articulates a simple premise: if an institution barely covers the amount it collectively spends, then that institution will not remain strong for long. Such erosion of financial standing and institutional positioning may occur gradually. And it may escape detection initially. Tight budgets may satisfy current operating needs. But they put off nonemergency spending such as facility maintenance, salary incentives for productive employees, and new programs that appeal to prospective students and families. Underbalanced but limited budgets and day-to-day spending keep the lights on and the institution functioning. Yet systematic reinvestment and reinvention cannot occur. The institution stagnates and its competitive standing erodes over time. Seemingly overnight, a college or university emerges from a trancelike state and stares at the unappetizing scenario of spending millions on deferred maintenance due to aging roofs, obsolete HVAC systems, and cracked asphalt on parking lots and walkways. Or they possess a stagnant curriculum of academic programs that lacks appeal. Such curriculum calcification, coupled with a Lazarus-like ability of faltering programs to stay alive, siphons funds away from needed alternatives. This combination lessens the institution's appeal in the eyes of prospective students, their families, and donors. Such a scenario convinces them to turn elsewhere. Revenues dry up. A gradual but inevitable downward spiral ensues.

Maryville's curriculum and teaching and learning techniques have been adapted greatly during the past decade. Its facilities have been continually improved and enhanced. No deferred maintenance exists. A list of future facilities needs has been formulated. Consistent annual surpluses—or margin—spur $5–7 million of annual institutional reinvestment.

Peter Benoist, the late respected and retired president of Enterprise Bank, served as chair of the board of trustees during the terms of two Maryville presidents, Pritchard and Lovin. He maintained that finances were clearly a priority for the board that became elevated under Dr. Lombardi. This emphasis was not just about generating more revenue. Its chief aim centered on providing funds to enhance the academic experience by smartly reinvesting in all areas of the institution.

Benoist candidly stated that higher education had not been an easy business for him to figure out. He noted that the challenges in higher education resemble those of banking: high fixed costs in terms of people and buildings; intense competition within the marketplace; a high degree of regulatory involvement from various local, state, and federal agencies; and technological innovations transforming how products are developed and distributed. Which industry was tougher in his view? "Higher education, frankly."

Benoist's successor, Tom Boudreau, has served as a trustee for the past two decades including a dozen as its chair. He echoes the mantra of "no margin, no mission" as justification to generate sustained operating surpluses that can be continually reinvested. Boudreau feels it is crucial for Maryville to keep asking itself whether various institutional programs are financially sustainable. The university must remain, in his view, mindful of the needs of major employers in the St. Louis and national communities such as his former employer,

Express Scripts (where he served as general counsel). Maryville needs to continue ongoing dialogue with these outside entities and keep asking, what do employers need from Maryville students? What do employers expect them to know when they graduate? What skills must they possess? Such an approach provides the framework for financially sustainable programs. It also enables students to possess knowledge that has true meaning in the real world and allows them to hit the ground running.

Jim Switzer, a lifelong St. Louis resident who is a retired executive with Emerson Electric, has led various trustee committees over the years since he first joined the board during the early 2000s. Among his roles has been his longtime stewardship of Maryville's Finance and Audit Committee. This perch has obviously provided him an inside perspective from which to assess the institution's financial practices.

When he became committee chair, Switzer worked very closely with CFO Larry Hays to develop reporting processes and systems that highlighted how Maryville was actually performing financially as opposed to old-style institutional accounting that Switzer contends "doesn't tell you anything about anything." With board support and cooperative effort from the administration, a sound financial underpinning for the institution was established.

This foundation has allowed the creative side of the institution to come to the fore, Switzer feels. The board has remained supportive of aggressively pursuing and achieving what he calls "conventional success." Enrollments have increased. So has the endowment. Consistent and positive operating results have been generated. Once Maryville achieved such conventional success, Switzer contends the institution has moved beyond to pursue "unconventional successes" in terms of personalized learning and technological innovation. Nobody on the board wanted to hunker down and be what Maryville already was previously once the finances were enhanced, according to Switzer. The board unanimously wanted Maryville to become something unique. But that process must start with a sound financial foundation, he emphasizes.

Switzer notes a few actions that are imperative for a college or university to implement when laying a strong financial foundation. First, an institution must generate positive financial returns through its routine operations. It cannot just keep adding programs, people, and facilities that do not contribute to and improve an institution's financial standing. Second, an institution needs to evaluate all its activities periodically to determine which ones bolster an institution financially and which ones require subsidy. Third, faltering programs must be pruned or eliminated.

The status quo does not prevail when weaknesses are detected. Maryville possesses the fortitude to act.

Maryville has shown a willingness to undertake these sometimes unappealing tasks. Its leadership has not shirked from the challenge of fostering change and trimming where necessary. The status quo does not prevail when weaknesses are detected. Maryville possesses the fortitude to act.

Maryville's financial reviews are conducted on a cash flow basis, according to Switzer. Forecasts are formulated by evaluating where the university will spend cash during a fiscal year compared to where cash will likely be generated. Switzer says Maryville simply looks at how much money will likely flow in and how much will likely flow out. At the end of the day, the university's overall financial goal is to have enough funds left over to reinvest robustly in new initiatives, especially academic ones; satisfy its debt obligations; maintain facilities and construct new ones, if deemed necessary; and underwrite other types of support systems to enhance student success such as life coaching.

Maryville expends great effort in understanding the cost side of its operations, Switzer emphasizes. Once that cost analysis is accomplished, comparisons are made against projected operating income. This continual analysis concerning operating costs is done largely to control overhead expenses. At most institutions, overhead expenses inexorably climb. Most college and universities seem resigned to this fate and do little to arrest or reverse this trend. Such increases consume an ever-larger portion of institutional budgets, shrink operating margins, and crowd out reinvestment. Maryville actually seeks to lessen its overhead expenses to free funds for whatever reinvestment is deemed most necessary.

The other institutional benefit of controlling overhead expenses pertains to tuition increases. Switzer points out that decreasing overhead expenses directly impacts the need to raise tuition. He notes that Maryville has actually frozen tuition levels for four of the last five years. For the 2020–2021 academic year, the university has actually enacted a 5 percent reduction for traditional undergraduate on-campus students. Maryville has done so largely through controlling its fixed, overhead costs. It allows Maryville to remain sensitive to the affordability of its students. The best way to ensure that an institution's students are not overwhelmed by student debt, Switzer contends, is by controlling all its costs—especially its fixed overhead—to keep its tuition flat or even lower it.

A SHREWD BUDGETING STRATEGY

The annual budgeting process at many institutions often remains oddly detached from its planning processes. Thus, financial expenditures may not match up well with designated institution-wide goals.

At many institutions, the process of developing an annual budget has become an exercise of drudgery that is anything but strategic and reflective of institutional goals. Little thought, discussion, or analysis accompanies its formulation. Hard choices between competing priorities are seldom debated or resolved. Resources are not allocated where they are most needed or can achieve the greatest results. Fiefdoms prove paramount as pockets of funds are set aside to appease internal constituencies. By the time all the funding is divvied up, there is little to nothing left to invest to achieve institution-wide goals.

The budget process at many institutions chugs along in much the same way from year to year—seemingly by inertia. Many of the individuals who serve on a budget committee view it largely as a nuisance. They may not fully engage in rigorous, thoughtful analysis—unless a suggestion is made to cut funding in their area of personal involvement. The process unfolds over many months highlighted by several desultory budget meetings until a balanced budget is formulated. Every campus constituency has seemingly enjoyed some special considerations. No one challenges its basic tenets from an institution-wide perspective. Little to no attention is given to how it will affect the institution's competitiveness in the marketplace.

A final budget document is approved by trustees. It keeps the institution operating for another year. Sighs of relief are breathed. Expressions of joy are heard from all. This task can be put aside for a few months before the next autopilot cycle kicks into gear. The ratified budget is usually balanced in the sense that revenues offset expenses to the penny. But this blueprint does not provide for strategic (re) investment. The planning and budget processes seemingly flounder on parallel tracks that never intersect.

A DYNAMIC ALIGNMENT OF PROCESSES

The planning and budgeting processes at Maryville remain deeply intertwined. They are anything but routine and lackluster. They seldom follow the exact same path one year to the next. To describe the process in another way, the financial budgeting process resembles a game of three-dimensional chess. Options are weighed from a variety of perspectives and viewpoints. Actions are evaluated according to likely outcomes. Moves happen only after careful consideration for how they will strategically position the institution in the future.

Maryville seeks to invest shrewdly and carefully to bolster its resources and extract maximum benefit. Such resources include its labor force, where continual investment in training is emphasized. The university also builds a large contingency and a series of smaller contingencies to maintain a financial cushion that can be tapped if an unforeseen opportunity arises or calamity occurs.

Hays, who served as Maryville's chief financial officer from 1982 to 2015, recalls there would be a lot of "crying and teeth gnashing" each year during the budget process. The biggest item in Maryville's budget, by far, is the cost associated with labor—including salaries and benefits. The better job the university can do in hiring the right people and matching these folks and their skills with the institution's strategic goals, according to Hays, the better off the institution will be operationally and financially.

Hays admits that before the Lombardi administration came to Maryville, there had been a tendency to hire new employees to assist struggling ones. Overhead costs climbed as a result. That tendency evaporated during the past decade as all employees were held account-able for performing their duties at a high level. If performance faltered, changes in personnel would result instead of increasing the number of staff. Overhead costs were kept in check by controlling the growth of the single biggest item of the university's budget while operational efficiency climbed.

Hays notes that while personnel costs comprise the largest share of the university budget, they tend not to vary greatly from year to year unless the university makes substantial changes in its programming or operations. Thus, departmental operating budgets must be evaluated carefully and thoughtfully. They should be adjusted from one year to the next as circumstances change. Careful management of operating costs, according to Hays, often spells the difference between an institution with a solid financial foundation and one with a much shakier financial base.

Hays knows that people must possess sufficient operating budgets to accomplish what they are supposed to do. But from the perspective of senior leadership, its job was to analyze overall spending patterns and make sure resources matched up well with the goals of the institution. Before the Lombardi era, the approach on the expenditure side was to take the previous year's budget and increase it by the inflation rate. There was not much scrutiny regarding how departments spent their money in the previous year or how much they had left over. As evidence, according to Hays, there were a number of years when lots of furniture showed up on Maryville's loading dock near the end of a fiscal year. Departments were purposely spending their remaining money on furnishings so they would have nothing left at year end. That practice no longer holds sway at Maryville.

New institutional budgeting techniques center on a zero-based model where all expenditures are evaluated from scratch as if in a completely new budget. Hays and his financial team began to scrutinize expenditures of all types, including how spending varied seasonally. Some departments would not spend much during the fall semester but would need to make significant expenditures in the spring because of their cycle of activities. Travel and attendance at conferences became a particular area of focus. Hays grew suspicious when lots of travel was undertaken toward the end of a fiscal year. Great effort was expended to trim certain categories of expenditures, such as travel expenses and office furnishings, without touching the muscle needed to accomplish the most important strategic goals.

TWO PRIMARY BENEFITS

That process of thoughtful analysis and close scrutiny accomplished two primary benefits, Hays contends. First, it saved dollars, lowered costs, and created space for some needed contingencies. Second, it changed the institutional culture. It forced people to match up resources with what they most needed to accomplish. That increased efficiency was multiplied and amplified on an accumulative basis from year to year. The budget process began to satisfy the needs of today while positioning the university well for the future.

Current Chief Financial Officer Steve Mandeville resides today in—of all places—Maryville, Illinois. It is literally no exaggeration when he says he lives and works at Maryville. He joined the university staff in June 2010 as assistant controller from BKD Public Accounting, which coincidentally performed Maryville's annual audit. Thus, he possessed more than a passing familiarity with Maryville's financial procedures and balance sheet before becoming an employee.

Mandeville was promoted to controller only eighteen months later. His ascension to chief financial officer came nearly three years after that when Hays retired. Mandeville's hiring and steady climb up Maryville's ranks has ensured a smooth transition in shepherding university finances.

A BUDGET PROCESS THAT LOOKS TO THE FUTURE

The annual budget process at Maryville seeks to preserve maximum flexibility. Because the institution's consistent enrollment growth among its traditional undergraduate, online, and adult populations has helped achieve substantial annual operating surpluses, Mandeville admits that he sometimes receives some pushback from certain individuals who question the need for controlled spending. These folks know it is highly likely that annual surpluses will ensue in due course. Thus, they resist scrutinizing expenditures closely.

Thoughtful spending decisions, though, allow Maryville to be flexible and impactful. The budget process represents a type of puzzle as it fits together. It is not always apparent what all the pieces will look like as it is assembled. That is why it is crucial to review all spending decisions so thoroughly—to provide financial leeway that can be leveraged if the right opportunities arise.

This annual budget process commences immediately after the October trustees meeting. It extends through April and wraps up in time for the spring trustees meeting when the final budget is presented and approved. It starts with an assessment of enrollment trends since tuition and fees account for more than 80 percent of Maryville's income. Enrollment estimates seek to determine reasonable projections for the following year. Factoring in likely investment and gift income with tuition projections, the institution determines a conservative projection for what its revenues will likely be.

Mandeville is quick to note that the institution resists adjusting or revising its revenue projections based on what expenses might total. The university never goes back and adjusts its revenue numbers. It never says, "If we increase our projections by fifty students, we can do this or that." Rather it develops what it considers conservative, realistic income projections.

Next the university looks at expenses. It begins with an analysis of strategic goals. Those items represent prioritized expenses for the upcoming fiscal year. Top priorities are identified and estimates are made of what it will take to resource them, Mandeville emphasizes. It starts with what he calls "the big rocks" that everyone designated as the priority goals. Those big items are allocated first. And then everything else falls out from there. The pot of remaining money indicates how much is available for the rest of the operating budget.

The university might decide that a program must be cut, or it might be put on hold, or it might be taken out for now but could possibly be considered in the future, Mandeville explains. The institution encourages a collaborative decision-making process with the President's Advisory Council (PAC) making necessary spending cuts and final decisions. Later in the fiscal year, when the university sees its actual results, it might opt to fund one or a few back burner items because enrollment or gifts exceeded expectations, or expenses remained lower than anticipated, or some combination of both. If ideas have merit and are deemed worthy—but not top—priorities, the university maintains them on a consideration list for when better than anticipated financial circumstances might allow for implementation.

Mandeville, like Hays, ensures that Maryville does not substantially factor endowment income into its operating budget. The institutional spending rate is 5 percent of a three-year rolling average. That amount is carefully analyzed each year, and its purpose is designated by the board. Is it needed for current spending on things like capital projects, or can it be left in the endowment? Or can a portion be spent while the rest is saved? Endowment income, thus, is not heavily relied upon to help balance the annual institutional operating budget.

BLUEPRINTS

One long-standing external partnership that Maryville University has maintained is with Credo, a higher education consulting firm with locations in North Carolina and Wisconsin. Credo, under Joanne Soliday, had initiated some consulting work at the direction of Maryville's board to develop a long-term strategic plan. Several months later, President Lombardi arrived on campus in the summer of 2007.

Soliday soon recognized that Maryville sought a much more distinctive and innovative path and that Lombardi was not afraid to push the innovation envelope. She correctly surmised that Maryville's path would be based, in large part, on a keen understanding of the market forces—especially technology—transforming higher education. Once this understanding had been inculcated within the university community and a common knowledge base established, the university could set clear goals, foster innovation, and allocate resources to navigate the shifting sands figuratively swirling around it. Extensive time and effort were expended in educating an educational community about the challenges buffeting the institution each day.

> **Maryville sought a much more distinctive and innovative path.**

Nowhere was this process more important than for the board of trustees. Composed of accomplished professionals chiefly from other industries, the board desired more than a nodding acquaintance with the issues confronting higher education. Members of the board unanimously gave Lombardi and his senior leadership team high marks concerning the way they educated both the board and the campus community. This process was both collaborative and challenging. Reading of articles and books preceded discussion and question and answer sessions. Tricky scenarios were debated. Various solutions were offered and critiqued. Soliday contends that the knowledge level of what is happening within higher education stands significantly higher at Maryville than it does at the majority of other schools she visits or works with. Knowledge is power, according to one old adage, and this baseline of common understanding has promoted robust dialogue, input, and buy-in from the Maryville community.

Soliday believes that the current strategic plan adopted by the board in February of 2015 is remarkable (See *Pivot: A Vision for the New University* written by Soliday and Lombardi and published by Advantage Media Group in 2019.) She points out that the university stands on the cutting-edge of innovation in all areas: daily operations, leadership development, putting the right people in the right places and retaining them, utilizing current technology to promote personalized learning that demonstrably maximizes student potential, and supporting student success at the highest levels for years beyond an individual's time on campus. These combined factors have led to Maryville becoming the fourth fastest growing private institution in 2018–2019 according to *The Chronicle of Higher Education.*

Maryville is not afraid of risk and moves more quickly than nearly all other schools Soliday sees. That type of environment is very appealing to employees in particular, she contends. This fact is often overlooked or dismissed elsewhere. Employees are the people who must translate and implement strategic priorities on a daily basis. A motivated and positive workforce is the best resource that any institution can possess and is a huge competitive advantage.

MARYVILLE'S CURRENT STRATEGIC PLAN

Maryville's current strategic plan spans from adoption in 2015 through 2022 when the university will celebrate its 150th anniversary.

The plan is audacious in its simplicity, including its choice of language and tight focus that is often lacking in such documents. It articulates just four main themes: active learning ecosystem, transformational innovation, diversity and inclusiveness, and strategic growth. A total of fifteen goals are spread under these four headings. Each goal is specific, measurable, and ambitious. Maryville must accomplish two goals a year to satisfy the aims of its plan. It is, thus, attainable.

Strategic plans often place their primary focus on aspirational language and aims that are not clear, realistic, or measurable. They often center on internal issues that are important to a campus community but irrelevant to those on the outside. Because of this scenario, these plans often fall short in providing any market-relevant enhancements. Such documents may make campus constituencies feel better in the short term because they serve as an institutional crutch of sorts. But as time passes and the pages of the calendar turn, symptoms lack proper diagnosis. Cures remain elusive. Nerves become frayed. Meaningful change hovers seemingly just beyond reach, much like Tantalus in Greek mythology perpetually and futilely reaching up for a bunch of grapes to satisfy his hunger or reaching down for a mouthful of water to quench his thirst.

Credo shares a philosophy with Maryville that strategic plans need to be agile and shifting over time. The current plan drew about 80 percent of its lifeblood from Maryville and 20 percent from Credo, according to Soliday. The partners have learned over time that together, they must develop strategy, line up initiatives consistent with that strategy in prioritized order, stay attentive that at the moment some initiatives are completed others must start, and recognize when an aim that previously seemed important is no longer relevant. Institutions cannot rely on a document that is set in stone with no changes allowed. An institution needs to keep asking: "What needs to be our strategy for the next several years, and what needs to be done this year? Let's move some things in and out of the priority list." A strategic plan must flow and adapt.

Most firms like Credo disappear from the scene once a strategic plan is approved by a board and distributed within a campus community. Implementation of a strategic plan lies strictly and exclusively with the school. Institutional focus soon tends to return to current issues. Planning for the future reverts to the back burner.

Not so at Maryville. Credo maintains ongoing contact and counsel. Soliday feels this collaboration has become increasingly strategic over time. Maryville has stepped to the forefront, and its deep leadership team has taken the lead in facilitating ongoing strategic planning. Soliday notes that when she is asked to visit Maryville's campus these days, it is largely to encourage people rather than to dispense advice. Maryville possesses a high degree of self-awareness and simply needs to maintain its enthusiasm and focus. Such progress is a great sign for the future of the institution in her view.

That Maryville has been able to keep much of its leadership team in place during the last decade is an accomplishment that should not be overlooked. Special attention has been paid to retention. A second or midlevel tier of emerging human talent has been acquired, designated, and groomed. Soliday estimates that only 3 percent of colleges have nurtured a second layer of leadership as strong as what Maryville possesses. Every vice president, according to her observations, has the time, energy, and opportunity to think and act strategically because the "bench" behind them is thick, talented, and trained. These vice presidents are able to look beyond their day-to-day challenges and focus on what hurdles are likely to emerge next. They also function together as a cohesive unit. They admittedly argue, fight, and bicker at times. Candor underscores their interactions. Sometimes someone gets their nose out of joint for a bit. At day's end, though, they pull together on the big, crucial issues.

The best presidential teams play in each other's sandboxes, Soliday contends. But they also have to have each other's backs. That is exactly what she sees from the team at Maryville. They play in each other's sandboxes without paranoia, without getting upset. Some particles get tossed around, and someone may grow momentarily irritated with another person. They ultimately realize, however, that they must all play together. And they always seem to have each other's backs when they leave a meeting room, no matter how high the temperature may have climbed inside during debate.

One strategy that Maryville has adopted that other institutions overlook or ignore concerns devoting sufficient time annually for long-range planning. The Maryville leadership team carves out a week's time each summer to leave campus, delve into deep discussions, and uncover hidden opportunities. Soliday says that most institutions Credo assists meet for only a few hours somewhere on campus once or twice a year to discuss long-term strategy. The focus of those discussions shifts to short-term concerns—everything that is currently wrong and what needs to be done to fix those problems. Instead, Maryville devotes substantial financial and human resources— and time—to tackle longer-term issues. The first day's agenda of a Maryville retreat might feature conversations about several short-term shortcomings that need to be addressed. However, focus soon shifts intensely and dramatically to look into the future for a sustained number of hours and days.

This time spent together away from campus fosters cohesion among the team, promoting familiarity, unity, and a common purpose. This sustained period of summer planning functions much like an NFL training camp, readying the team for the short-term obstacles and long-term rigors. A deep bench of able players is identified and cultivated. Roles are adapted and then adopted. The Maryville leadership team returns to campus with a fresh perspective and an altered focus—devoted as much to addressing long-term opportunities as short-term concerns. Maryville has found that the substantial resources allocated each summer to this sustained period of reflection and renewal are worth it. This period of intense focus has helped position the university to assume the lead role in planning for its own future—an institutional skill far from universal within higher education, according to Credo.

> **A deep bench of able players is identified and cultivated.**

MARYVILLE'S BRANDING

How can the brand identity of any institution best be described? Some folks contend that brand identity represents the sum total of the attributes that come to mind when an individual hears the name of an entity, place, or product. Such brand identity incorporates both the factual and emotional attributes of a brand—whether accurate or not. A brand name tangibly exists because people see it printed on a package, on an electronic screen, or on a banner or sign. But brand identity truly exists only in an individual's heart and mind. Thus, branding represents the process of creating and disseminating a name with the goal of developing a favorable identity. Advertising icon David Ogilvy termed it "the intangible sum of a product's attributes."

Effective branding differentiates places or products from those of competitors. Branding in higher education should serve this purpose. But distinctions often can become blurred. Many higher education institutions tend to act much like zebras on the plains of Africa.

Every zebra, as you may know, has a distinct stripe pattern. No two zebras look the same. Yet when they cluster together, their distinction disappears.

Zoologists explain that zebras cluster together to help ward off attacks by predators. Unfortunately for higher education institutions, such clustering makes them more susceptible—not less—to attacks from others looking to poach their students, faculty, and donors. Distinctions between institutions become faint. Brand identity becomes less and less apparent. Advocates, over time, feel less and less compelled to demonstrate their loyalty and support for an institution that appears increasingly commonplace.

Each institution, like each zebra, is distinctive: possessing its own attributes. Yet many institutions tend to focus the bulk of their efforts to match the attributes of others, thereby blurring with other similar institutions in the minds of customers. Their institutional distinctiveness lessens. Colleges and universities often emulate the offerings and facilities of other institutions composing their peer group rather than identifying and cultivating features that help them stand out. They end up camouflaging themselves among a herd.

Maryville has successfully moved beyond this herd mentality. Like a lone zebra, it has concentrated on featuring its own distinctive stripes. The university has thus achieved a higher profile and more distinctive brand identity within the St. Louis community and beyond.

ACTING ON NEW PRIORITIES

When Mark Lombardi arrived on campus in the summer of 2007, he agreed with the board that enhancing Maryville's visibility and brand recognition should be a top institutional priority. No longer would Maryville be considered a best kept secret.

The university, fortunately, had already laid some firm building blocks. None was more important than a step taken during Keith Lovin's presidency when Maryville had become the lead sponsor of the St. Louis Speakers Series. Each year, this series brings seven famous speakers to St. Louis, including people such as President Clinton, Robert Redford, Jane Goodall, David McCullough, and Condoleezza Rice. This sponsorship promoting discussion about issues of contemporary importance remains completely consistent with Maryville's mission as a center of thought and ideas. The Speakers Series has raised the university's visibility within the surrounding community and provided an ideal opportunity for the institution to cultivate close relationships with individual donors and/or alumni who enjoy having the coveted chance to attend a private dinner and undertake dialogue with the speakers.

No longer would Maryville be considered a best kept secret.

Building on that success, Lombardi joined the St. Louis Sports Commission in 2010, and shortly thereafter, Maryville began working closely with the commission to become the presenting sponsor for the Musial Awards, which are prominent awards that celebrate sportsmanship in the United States. Now nationally televised, this awards show highlights the values of sportsmanship and fair play that Stan Musial personified. Recipients include athletes like Hank Aaron and Arnold Palmer. This platform has greatly increased awareness of Maryville in St. Louis and beyond.

To solidify this progress, Vice President for Integrated Marketing & Communications Marci Sullivan turned for branding help to Fred Cisneros, a talented graphic designer from Santa Fe, New Mexico. Together they provided the final human piece of the puzzle regarding Maryville's quest to frame a more prominent brand and reputation.

Lombardi and Sullivan charged Cisneros and his firm with creating a new brand identity, including a logo, for the university. As context, please bear in mind that many university logos lack distinction and are rooted in campus landmarks that are unfamiliar to external audiences. Cisneros Design set to work to provide distinctive and impactful concepts for consideration that would attract positive attention. Brainstorming ensued. Some sessions between Cisneros Design and Maryville occurred face-to-face while others occurred remotely via Skype. Work started with the logo. Some basic parameters were set by the Maryville leadership. The new logo would have to be an *M*, it had to be red, and it had to have a bold, strong feel associated with it. This symbol had to have a contemporary look, be flexible when implemented across all platforms, and translate well among varied audiences. Such characteristics, it was felt, would reflect the vibrant future that Maryville sought.

Cisneros Design welcomed such parameters. True creativity begins with limits, Cisneros contends. When a client tells you what they want, it defines the ultimate goal but it does not necessarily limit what options are available to achieve that goal. Guidelines evolved over the nine months regarding what could be done with the logo and how it could be used. The group also settled on a new tagline of "Maryville. Many Connections. One U." This theme acknowledges the university's investment in technology and connectivity within an emerging digital world.

Cisneros Design worked incessantly throughout 2015 with Maryville to execute the new brand identity. Ultimately, the firm produced a logo that is unique in higher education. Sleek and professional, yet corporate and cutting edge, the Maryville *M* has become a staple within the St. Louis community and increasingly on the national stage.

Cisneros admits his delight in seeing how Maryville's new brand identity has come to fruition and taken root. He marvels at how the Maryville community, after a few initial reservations, rallied behind the platform and executed it so well. Cisneros Design's own website prominently features this project under the heading: "A brand that became a culture." Both the new logo and brand platform reflect elegance, beauty, and concision. That combination is never easy to pull off. It demonstrates that simplicity—rather than complexity—offered an effective solution. It also showed that the university's conception of basic parameters of its brand identity facilitated the development of a new system.

It is not just the current members of the campus community who have embraced the new look. Daylene Litchenwalter graduated in 1986 from Maryville's interior design program. As someone artistically inclined, she has taken notice of the new *M* during a campus visit and while reading the university's website and magazine. She agrees that it looks more contemporary: "It is just bolder!"

Such admiration also extends to the generation of Maryville alumni who attended the former campus in south St. Louis. Elizabeth Searles graduated in 1960 with a degree in English literature. After the Maryville campus relocated to West County, she worked with her husband, Michael, and others to salvage artifacts from the old location for display at the new one. When asked to comment about the current campus, the first thing she said was: "I like the big, red *M*. I like all the new signage. It makes the place seem energetic and modern." Such sentiments are echoed by Judy Luepke, who graduated in 1958 with a degree in education: "I am thrilled when I come to this campus. I just love the new *M* symbol. It's all over the place."

Cisneros offers some final thoughts on the new brand identity. Maryville has taken its brand identity so much further than imagined ten years ago, he states. The higher education landscape is pretty conservative and cautious by nature, he contends. Institutions do not necessarily take the risk of being bold and thinking about their target audiences. In general, there are a lot of missed opportunities in higher education marketing, to his mind. Maryville seized its opportunities aggressively and now reaps the benefits of its commitment and clear thinking.

Sullivan concurs regarding the results but offers a varied perspective concerning its evolution. She points out that while it is a new brand platform, it reflects the Maryville of yesteryear that was built on a solid foundation of academic rigor. There are few instances of greater difficulty for someone in her position, she emphasizes, than trying to modify public perceptions based on negative connotations. Building a brand from a position of strength, as Maryville did, is much easier than trying to alter public perception. She feels the new brand identity helps Maryville tell compelling, visual stories to varied key audiences such as business executives and high school guidance counselors. Those audiences are the ones, she notes, who will hire Maryville graduates, send their children to Maryville, and engage with the institution as community partners.

RIGOROUS RESEARCH AND DATA ANALYTICS

It is always a challenge to ensure that the university is efficient and consistent in how it communicates about the institution, Sullivan continues. Maryville has brand ambassadors among its students, faculty, and alumni. One of her primary focus areas in the future is to ensure that the university's strong brand promise is upheld. That goal entails rigorous research and data analytics to ensure that Maryville has met the standards of its brand promise.

Such measurements to gauge effectiveness are easier to accomplish in some areas than others. In digital formats, it is relatively simple to run reports that measure activity to assess return on investment. Which digital ads generate the highest number of leads? How many website visitors find a site and how do they utilize its content? How many web visitors ultimately apply for admission? Are numbers of social media followers and "likes" increasing over time?

Such measurements are not so simple to formulate elsewhere. Since the rollout of its new brand identity platform, Maryville has devoted additional funding to promoting the overall image of the institution. Some folks might call these efforts "traditional advertising." One prominent example is the large *M* logo that adorns the centerfield scoreboard at St. Louis Cardinals games in Busch Stadium. Another is the university's sponsorship arrangement with the National Hockey League's St. Louis Blues franchise. This agreement offers a variety of promotional opportunities—including introducing starting lineups on nationwide television during the 2019 Stanley Cup playoffs. A third opportunity one could point to is a five-year naming sponsorship for a new ice arena in nearby Chesterfield located prominently along interstate Highway 64. This arena, located a short drive from campus, will serve as the home facility for the university's ice hockey program.

It is obviously much harder to pin down and evaluate the efficacy of these types of marketing assets on a cost-benefit basis than it is in digital formats. But they have undoubtedly increased the university's name recognition in traditional local markets as well as within new regional and national ones.

Sullivan notes that Maryville completed an awareness survey in 2016 benchmarked against 2013. Results indicate that Maryville enjoys a significantly higher level of awareness and favorable reputation, particularly among the general public. She points to an 11 percent increase in web traffic resulting from individuals who conduct an organic search—when one types Maryville's name directly into a search box rather than through a referral from another website or a search engine like Google. Maryville incessantly touts its high career placement rate of 98 percent within its brand platforms to underscore the value and validity of a Maryville education.

Ashlee Brockenbrough earned her bachelor's degree in English from Maryville in 2012, followed by an MBA in 2016. She was a distinguished student-athlete competing in volleyball; she later coached the Maryville women's team. Brockenbrough served her alma mater in a number of areas—enrollment, advancement, athletics, and integrated marketing and communications—before departing for a corporate career. She reflects on the greater visibility that Maryville has achieved since her association with the institution a decade ago. She said, "Not too many years ago, Maryville was still referred to as the best kept secret in St. Louis." But Maryville has since taken varied and important steps to become increasingly known as a local, regional, and national presence as demonstrated by benchmarks.

At the end of the day, it is obvious that several factors fell into place at Maryville to allow it to achieve greater name recognition and enhanced brand equity. In brief, they include the following:

It all started with the solid foundation laid more than 140 years ago to ensure the highest level of academic rigor.

This solid base was then combined with an awareness of marketing opportunities that were consistent with Maryville's clearly articulated institutional mission.

Finally, blended into that mix was a proclivity for creativity coupled with an appreciation for differentiation that ensured a recipe for success.

ATHLETICS, WRESTLING, AND ESPORTS

Enhanced name recognition flowing from a college or university's athletic programs customarily translates into institutional success in several ways. Media exposure rises, visitors to flagship websites climb, and social media followers increase. All of these factors result in higher numbers of applicants for admission. In a similar vein, alumni feel more pride toward their alma mater because of the buzz resulting from athletics. Such pride typically increases alumni philanthropic support. Likewise, contributions from other types of donors rise as well. Therefore, institutions possessing a higher public profile—and a track record of athletic success devoid of unfavorable incidents— tend to garner greater levels of philanthropic support. Finally, the excitement created throughout the campus surrounding an institution's athletic prowess enhances student life, personal enjoyment, and engenders a unique excitement in many attending the school. All these factors together translate into fiscal and institutional success.

Athletics has long played a significant role in Maryville University's daily life, stretching back more than a half century to its days as an all-girls school located within its diminutive, southside St. Louis campus. Many alumni who attended the original campus still speak with enthusiasm regarding the active role that athletics played at the old Maryville. Although the original campus did not feature a large number of acres, it offered outdoor facilities for soccer, tennis, and field hockey. It also featured a gymnasium for basketball. And it wasn't just students who enjoyed athletics. Sister Patricia Barrett, a renowned professor who taught popular courses in government, routinely donned tennis shoes and hiked up the hems of her habit while defeating various comers who dared to challenge her on the tennis courts.

Intercollegiate athletics, though, was not yet a prominent focus when the institution relocated in the early 1960s. However, the new campus offered substantial acreage that could accommodate the development of varied athletic facilities for women's squads competing against other institutions. Men's athletic teams later followed.

One observer who brings a long-term viewpoint regarding Maryville athletics is Lonnie Folks. Folks graduated in 1982 with a bachelor's degree in business and earned an MBA in 1998. He played soccer and baseball as an undergraduate. After an employment stint of a few months at IBM after graduation, Folks returned to campus and served for years in a variety of administrative and coaching positions.

His enduring contributions to the institution's athletic programs are recognized through the annual Lonnie Folks Award, given to a deserving recipient who embodies the "loyalty, character, dedication, and positive attitude modeled by Lonnie Folks as a student-athlete, coach, sports information director, and athletics administrator at Maryville University."

Folks says, "If I were talking to someone about Maryville, I would say that Maryville really gives you an opportunity to explore being who you think you want to be. That's true whether or not you are a student-athlete. That's exactly what Maryville was for me. It's big enough and still growing, so you feel as if you're part of a campus community. You get to do a lot of collegial things, but it's still small enough that the president of the school can know you by name."

SUCCESS IN MANY SPORTS

The university's teams, which compete under the nickname "Saints," took root, grew, and prospered. Maryville became one of six charter members of the NCAA Division III St. Louis Intercollegiate Athletic Conference (SLIAC). Facilities were upgraded and expanded. It achieved success in many sports during the next two decades in the SLIAC. These accomplishments were capped by the women's basketball team, garnering an all-time NCAA Division III record of ninety-three consecutive regular season conference wins in 2008. By that point, though, explorations had begun regarding the possibility of upgrading Maryville athletics to NCAA II and joining the Great Lakes Valley Conference (GLVC). This step would provide enhanced competition, visibility, and a larger geographic footprint throughout the upper Midwest.

The move to NCAA Division II was not without its risks. First, NCAA Division II requires the awarding of athletics scholarships to student-athletes, a situation prohibited under NCAA Division III guidelines. That change would require Maryville University to devote greater financial resources to athletics. Others fretted that regular, extended GLVC journeys would also require greater institutional financing for travel and lodging. Second, many faculty members worried that the academic performance of student-athletes might suffer. They were concerned that scholarship athletes competing at a higher and more demanding level while also traveling greater distances from campus would lag behind in the classroom. Finally, administrators and coaches wondered if Maryville would be able to recruit enough accomplished athletes to compete successfully in the GLVC while maintaining the high academic standards required of all Maryville student-athletes.

Maryville moved quickly but carefully to assess its options. On the one hand, there were risks and challenges associated with moving to NCAA Division II and the GLVC. At the same time, there were risks associated with remaining in NCAA Division III within the SLIAC. Many of that conference's schools were rural institutions whose viability had become increasingly precarious.

When Mark Lombardi had interviewed with Maryville's board of trustees in 2007, the careful expansion of Maryville's geographic footprint beyond Missouri and southern Illinois to new markets was deemed a top institutional priority. The GLVC featured schools located in markets from Kansas City to Indianapolis, Cincinnati, and Chicago. It seemed that integrating Maryville's athletic teams into the GLVC would provide enhanced exposure and name recognition that could be leveraged to boost enrollment, alumni outreach, and financial support. Maryville performed a detailed cost-benefit analysis. Options were compared. Soon thereafter, senior campus leadership recommended to its board of trustees the move to NCAA Division II and the GLVC. The board unanimously ratified this plan. Within the year, Maryville had left the SLIAC and NCAA Division III and joined the GLVC and NCAA Division II.

One accomplished student-athlete from that time, Abby Deuthman Blackstock, remembers the transition vividly. Recruited from across the state of Missouri from Kansas City, she graduated in 2013 with a sports business degree. Blackstock knew she would be part of the first Maryville class of student-athletes transitioning to Division II. The level of on-court competition was initially tough to match her first year, but slowly and surely, the team improved. She reflects that "blazing this path was both fun and exciting!" She and her teammates welcomed the chance to play new teams with fine athletes located beyond Missouri and southern Illinois.

"The biggest difference between Division II and Division III is the time a student-athlete devotes to their sport," she contends. "Division II represents the perfect middle ground because it is very competitive and time-consuming, but a student-athlete still is able to retain enough free time to pursue

> studies and other activities. It represents a balance of time and interests. In Division I, your time is tightly controlled for you, and other interests are limited."

She admits that Division III is great because there are very passionate people who are not on scholarship but play because they love their sport. But the level of competition is uneven because there is no scholarship involved. She thinks that Maryville handled the transition very well and that competing in Division II has benefited the university in many ways.

Blackstock's contention is based in fact. In her junior year, Maryville won the GLVC's women's basketball championship in its first year of eligibility after transitioning into Division II. The following year, her final year of athletic eligibility, she received recognition as GLVC Player of the Year, second team All-American, and a scholar-athlete. She completed her career as the school's all-time leading scorer (1,463 points) and rebounder (633 rebounds).

TARGETING NEW SPORTS

Maryville's leadership had compiled a list of target sports to add if the right opportunity came along. But it would be crucial to pursue such new sports prudently. Maryville had to be certain it could provide the proper infrastructure, resources, and academic support for each new team. Wrestling stood high on that target list of additional sports. Its appearance there would prove providential.

Mike Denny has achieved a record of success in college coaching that only John Wooden and a few others might not envy. As head wrestling coach at University of Nebraska-Omaha for thirty-two years, his squads finished in the top five in the nation twenty-seven times while earning seven national championships. That total is the highest in NCAA Division II wrestling history. In 2005, his team achieved the unprecedented feat of winning the national competitive championship while also securing the national academic championship. That squad remains the only wrestling team in Division II history to do so. It is hard to argue that Denny's teams were not doing things the right way, evidenced by their achievements in the classroom and on the mat.

The 2011 season ended with customary success as Denny's squad secured the NCAA Division II wrestling championship. The final round was contested across state in Kearney, Nebraska. Denny's team had an avid following there. Thus, after the final match, a throng of alumni, boosters, parents, and team members packed a room at the host hotel to celebrate. While speaking to the assembled folks, Denny noticed that his cell phone kept vibrating in his pocket. He concluded his remarks. As soon as time allowed, he checked his device. He noticed a voice mail message from his new athletic director, who had been at the school for less than a year. He had seldom, if ever, called Denny before. The coach assumed he wished to offer his congratulations.

Denny returned the call. He was then informed the university had decided to drop both football and wrestling that very morning. The university chancellor, who had approved this decision, had attended the matches in Kearney but said nothing about the decision while posing in team photos celebrating the victory. Denny called him to inquire. The chancellor confirmed the decision. Denny was told the university had made a decision to move into NCAA Division I as a member of the Summit League. This conference did not have wrestling. Thus, his program was abruptly terminated.

Denny struggled to determine what next steps to take. He knew of no precedent. In the meantime, he had received more than eight hundred supportive calls. These messages filled his cell and office phones. That Monday, alone in his office, he remembers, "I put my hands on my head and prayed that someone would provide an opportunity to resurrect my program."

Maryville's then Vice President of Enrollment Jeffrey D. Miller saw a story that same morning explaining that the reigning Division II national wrestling championship team had been dropped by its home institution. Miller knew that wrestling sat high on Maryville's list of desired sports. Why not try to land a national champion? He immediately placed a call to Denny's cell phone. Funnily enough, Denny picked up the call only because he knew that there was no longer any room for more messages.

Miller explained who he was, what institution he represented, and asked if he could come to Omaha to talk to him about an opportunity to move his wrestling program to Maryville. Denny was stunned. He kept asking Miller who he was and why he was calling, suspecting that someone might be playing a cruel joke on him. Years later, in retrospect, Miller admits it still gives him chills when he reflects that two strangers in two different geographic locations would use the same word—opportunity—moments apart to underscore a fledgling partnership.

Eventually Denny agreed to an Omaha visit from Miller, who met all the assistant coaches and wrestlers. Miller then organized a team visit to St. Louis. The Omaha contingent could see Maryville's campus; talk to faculty, staff, and students; and sample the St. Louis metropolitan area.

Maryville determinedly cleared several hurdles before announcing at a subsequent campus press conference that they would initiate a wrestling program the next season led by a Hall of Fame coach. This news generated national coverage on ESPN and included a mention in *The Wall Street Journal*, a publication that Denny admits he never expected his name to appear in. President Lombardi, meanwhile, was flooded with email messages of support from throughout the wrestling community across the nation.

The entire transfer process for the wrestling program had taken four weeks. Eight Omaha wrestlers joined their coach in St. Louis. He set to work recruiting others to supplement his squad for the next year. Practice space was freed up in, of all places, the university library by converting a square, multipurpose space into a wrestling facility that included showers and a locker room. Mats were purchased for meets to be held in the gymnasium of the Simon Athletic Center. A few months later, some preseason polls ranked Maryville's wrestling team as a national contender in NCAA Division II for the upcoming season even though it had yet to contest its first match.

Miller reflects that Maryville had just joined Division II when he ventured to Omaha. Bringing in a Hall of Fame coach with a handful of his nationally successful student-athletes raised the bar tremendously. When the university attracted such successful people, many other good things seemed to happen along the way. The decision helped the university achieve greater recognition and national exposure. Miller does not know anywhere else he has worked where he would pick an athletics story as his favorite professional memory, but this story ranks as his once in a career opportunity.

Denny's wrestlers have also continued to excel in the classroom as evidenced by his 2018–2019 squad finishing first in the national academic wrestling championship. They have achieved on the mats as well. One of the original eight wrestlers who transitioned from Omaha to St. Louis, Matt Baker, became Maryville's first NCAA Division II national champion in the 197-pound classification. He garnered recognition as a first team Academic All-American as well.

Baker still marvels at the warm reception he received at Maryville. He contends that Maryville provided the perfect fit for him and other student-athletes who came from Omaha or joined the program after its establishment in St. Louis. He credits Maryville's academic staff with working cooperatively with him to recognize his academic work at University of Nebraska-Omaha in a way that allowed him to earn an undergraduate degree in biology followed by a fourteen-month program in secondary education that permitted him to secure his master's degree as well. Nate Rodriguez has followed in Baker's footsteps and became Maryville's second NCAA Division II national champion in the 141-pound classification.

NEW SPORTS FACILITIES

Enhancing athletic facilities are an ongoing institutional goal. Maryville has built a new lacrosse, softball, and tennis facility along with a new soccer stadium and baseball park. It has additional plans for all other sports and undertook construction of the Maryville Hockey Arena in 2019 in partnership with the city of Chesterfield.

Saints athletics accolades have continued to pile up, starting with the GLVC presenting the Maryville Saints with its 2014–2016 James R. Spalding Sportsmanship Award. And most importantly, Maryville has won the NCAA President's Award for Academic Excellence for five consecutive years, including in 2015 as the only university in America with a 100 percent graduation rate for all its student-athletes.

ESPORTS AT MARYVILLE

Another success story pertains to the university's ESports team. ESports, for those who are not familiar with the term, is a form of gaming utilizing sophisticated computers. It has achieved enormous popularity around the globe, due in no small part to sports network ESPN's decision to televise it live. ESports remains under consideration as an Olympic sport for the upcoming 2024 Games.

John Lewington, a longtime Maryville faculty member in the John E. Simon School of Business, recalls his introduction to ESports. A young man named Dan Clerke came to him for academic advice. Clerke admitted he was not spending much time studying because he had a business, ESports. Lewington asked him to elaborate because he had a $2,000 scholarship available for student entrepreneurs. Lewington wondered if Maryville might consider beginning its own ESports team. Clerke, Lewington, and Lombardi met together, and the young man firmly pronounced that if Maryville allowed him to recruit an ESports team, it would go undefeated and win the collegiate national championship for League of Legends in its first year. And that is exactly what happened! Maryville went 49–0 that first season in 2015 and won the national championship. Maryville subsequently became one of the first universities in the country to offer scholarships to ESports participants. The Maryville squad captured its third of four national championships in Los Angeles in 2019 and finished second to China in the World Championships in July of that year.

Maryville is now recognized as the Alabama of ESports and is part of the inaugural collegiate ESports association. With two ESports team of ten players each along with an additional fifty students engaged in the club sport, ESports has placed Maryville on the national stage of this emerging sports phenomenon.

PHASE II

DISRUPTIVE REVOLUTION

"Nimble" is the word that members of the Maryville community use most often when asked to list university characteristics. More than one hundred extended interviews with Maryville staff, faculty, alumni, community members, trustees, and students reveal this fact. Examples of the university acting nimbly form a common theme that weaves throughout this narrative. That trait is normally not a characteristic associated with universities and how they operate. Specific examples show how Maryville acts to seize opportunities that appear in only a narrow time frame, all requiring a concerted institutional focus.

DECISIONS, DECISIONS

Why is Maryville University an outlier in many respects? One explanation is that the university consciously adopts a highly expeditious pace in its decision-making. But does that mean Maryville is rash or does not carefully consider the ramifications of new policies, procedures, or programs? Absolutely not.

Retired Vice President Jerry Brisson contends that at Maryville, **deliberation is more about *intense* focus than it is about time spent.**

Decisions result from thorough analysis and comprehensive review of issues. But that process does not equate to taking extended amounts of time. Unlike many, if not most, institutions of higher learning, issues do not get bogged down in bureaucracies and campus committees meandering along for month after month, year after year.

The key to this approach is anticipation. Maryville has its own "R & D" division made up of a loose collection of faculty, staff, and community members who research and analyze options before they present themselves. When opportunity knocks, much of the analysis has already occurred. What is emphasized is a laser-like, intense focus on an issue—a thorough analysis and decision completed quickly and with a carefully planned implementation.

Brisson notes that those individuals involved in evaluating the relative merits of a particular issue are expected to give concerted focus, study it comprehensively and quickly, and play an active part at PAC during deliberations of pros and cons. If PAC decides more information is needed, one is expected to find that information and bring the issue back expeditiously for further evaluation. Issues are not allowed to linger or simmer on the back burner for long. Decisions are made to proceed ahead or move in a different direction. Uncertainty does not hang in the air or clutter the agenda.

In contrast, at so many other institutions—by the time a decision is finally made and implementation starts—the slow, lumbering process may mean the designated solution may no longer be appropriate. By the time the diagnosis has been made and the treatment administered, the ailment may no longer be the same. Complications may have changed the situation. And the institution may have maneuvered so cautiously and slowly that it fails to realize it and adapt accordingly. Maryville has sidestepped this trap of equating extended timeframes with sound decision-making.

THE THREE-LEGGED STOOL

Vice President for Integrated Marketing and Communications Marcia Sullivan cites a "three-legged stool" of action that underscores the university's desired pace of operation. The "three legs" strategy requires that Maryville:

▶ Anticipates issues, trends, and problems as soon as possible and even before they occur;

▶ Pays attention to detail both when evaluating new ideas and programs and during implementation;

▶ Acts with a sense of urgency.

"Just like a startup company, we believe in moving quickly, very nimbly," Lombardi says. "Our office of strategic information is constantly analyzing the market, workforce trends and issues, labor statistics, et cetera. We're not reacting; we're proactive."

Sullivan confesses the difficulty of simultaneously keeping all three legs steady and secure. She admits there are very few individuals who can manage all three of those steps at any given time. But that is why the Maryville community efficiently operates together as a high-performance team. One or two individuals are in the anticipation mode; another subset is more detail-oriented, focused on analytics, and drilling down into the details; and another contingent—and Sullivan usually consider herself within this camp—creates a sense of urgency and understands that timing is important. It is those collective steps of executing well in all three categories that has kept the Maryville ship righted, on course, and moving quickly. She believes this mindset has helped create the framework for action that has made a lot of the success to date possible.

SHARED GOVERNANCE

Most higher education institutions operate on a model of shared governance. This term seems to mean different things to different people. According to a 2009 article in *The Chronicle of Higher Education* by Gary A. Olson, shared governance represents a delicate balance between faculty and administration. On the one hand, both parties participate in planning and decision-making while, on the other hand, they ensure institutional accountability and promote efficiency and effectiveness.

Bear in mind that the actual legal authority in nearly all colleges and universities originates from one place: a governing board. The board hires the president and delegates day-to-day responsibility to him or her, who may, in turn, delegate certain authority to other officials, normally regarding particular issues or administrative units. So the power to make and implement decisions can be diffuse.

Over time, shared governance has come to mean an increased number of constituencies participating in all decision-making processes with the illusionary goal of consensus. If that sounds like a prescription for cumbersome and torturous deliberation, the honest answer is yes, exactly. The notion of consensus being a primary goal of shared governance has served to hinder change, slow down, or, in many cases, strangle progress, and it is one of the key factors in the decline of higher education in this digital age. One key element of shared governance, however, needs to be kept in mind: the concept does not require all campus constituencies to be involved in every phase of decisions. Certain constituencies or individuals may be asked to share expertise or ideas at a particular juncture, but participation at one stage does not guarantee a role in the formulation of a final decision. Shared governance does not mean that decision-making must proceed slowly for an institution to achieve success.

As Olson wrote in his *Chronicle* article about shared governance: "No one person is arbitrarily making important decisions absent the advice of key constituents; nor is decision-making simply a function of a group vote. The various stakeholders participate in well-defined parts of the process. The second, but overlapping, concept is that certain constituencies are given primary responsibility over decision-making in certain areas." So, to illustrate, faculty exercise primary responsibility over curriculum matters at most institutions.

Maryville University seems to have struck the shared governance balance better than many other higher education institutions. Rather than competing fiefdoms jealously guarding every blade of turf they perceive as their own and fighting to the death to protect that terrain, collaboration normally tends to prevail. Requests are formulated in divisions across the university—including academics, student life/ success, facilities, etc. They are filtered to the President's Advisory Council where most key institutional decisions are made. Others— usually major financial and strategic decisions—may flow from the president (and PAC) to the board of trustees for a final decision.

PAC has been expanded in recent years from seven vice presidents to a team of fifteen, made up of vice presidents, deans, and others who earn a place at the table based on their ability, areas of expertise, results they have achieved, and their overarching commitment to the vision of Maryville. As part of this structure, other campus experts are pulled into a PAC meeting to provide additional perspectives for the group to consider. PAC has been mindful, though, not to let its larger membership hinder its ability to act as quickly as possible.

Members of PAC seem to recognize their balanced role in representing a department's needs while assessing the lasting impact of a policy on the university overall. PAC members are encouraged to transmit information gleaned from their various administrative units to the group and, thereby, up the chain of command. Likewise, all members acknowledge that an important part of their job entails explaining PAC deliberations and decisions that others need to know about and understand. As mentioned earlier, intense focus rather than long periods of deliberation remains the hallmark of Maryville decision-making.

A COURAGEOUS MINDSET

One-time dean of Maryville's College of Arts and Sciences and now Vice President of Academic Affairs Cherie Fister has served for than twenty years on the Maryville faculty. She notes, "One of the major changes that I have seen in the past ten years is that as an institution, Maryville has upped its game, raised its profile, and heightened expectations across the board." In the best way, she sees the university as a highly ambitious institution. Fister feels that Maryville has always been a fine institution that has done very well by its students. But she sees a different energy now. She believes that change is a great compliment to the school's heritage and what it has always been. She discerns an innovative liveliness percolating through all programs that makes for a very exciting place.

Her predecessor, Mary Ellen Finch, has remained a fixture at Maryville in varying capacities since 1974. Once the dean of the School of Education, she retired for the first time from that role almost thirty years ago in 1988. But her passion for education and Maryville brought her back in a variety of other roles, including leading Maryville's physical therapy program, filling in as the interim dean of its School of Health Professions, and establishing its Center for Teaching and Learning. Ultimately, she was tapped by Lombardi to serve as vice president of academic affairs in 2008, a post she held with vibrant energy into the summer of 2018.

Finch traces an enduring institutional commitment to risk-taking and personalized education to the Sisters of the Sacred Heart. It has threaded its way through to the present day, permeating the ethos of the campus community and especially the Maryville faculty. Finch contends that the university has taken risks when others have shied away. One of her prime examples: the uprooting of the physical campus from south St. Louis and relocating it to then rural West County. That move was considered risky—some called it idiotic—when the decision was made. Yet it has proved a master stroke of foresight in providing an expansive, convenient, and congenial home base.

That courageous mindset continues to influence institutional decision-making. Finch contends that the President's Advisory Council (PAC) senior leadership team features innovators and risk-takers that also work together as a cohesive unit. She cites the willingness to move forward without endless hesitation and deliberation and say, "Sure, we will do that but do so carefully." At the same time, the university does not go out on a limb regarding budgeting and finances. **The interesting and most noteworthy contrast is that the university is a risk-taker programmatically but remains conservative fiscally.** The university budgets frugally so it has the latitude to take risks and try something new. Funds are invested carefully—where they are most required—while all expenses are monitored closely.

Faculty members continue to exercise primary authority over the curriculum while engaging in a series of working groups built around driving the goals of the strategic plan. Groups such as Digital Transformation, Active Learning Ecosystem, Life Coaching K–12 Partnership, Student Experience, Access and Opportunity, Growth and Emerging Careers, and Partnerships represent more than seventy-five faculty and staff who meet and develop action items to enhance and accelerate each area's goals. Those ideas are then vetted by PAC for action and implementation. Given that Maryville's growth over the past fourteen years has allowed it to increase the percentage of faculty by 55 percent (180) and staff by 34 percent (350) means that a growing reservoir of talent and new ideas has infused Maryville's strategic plan keeping it fresh, cutting edge, and futuristic.

CONNECTIVITY

Maryville has made a concerted effort to upgrade its information technology (IT) capabilities and infrastructure. Jerry Brisson recognized that need when he joined Maryville as vice president for planning, research, and technology in 2007. Brisson was well suited to deal with such challenges. A calm New Englander who once taught high school English for a decade before migrating to college administration, Brisson assessed Maryville's IT capabilities from a 30,000-foot perspective with a keen eye on the emergence of digitization and what it may mean for the future of education. His analysis would focus on the type and amount of resources—human, technical, and financial—that would be needed to transform and revolutionize living and learning technology at Maryville.

During his first few months, Brisson focused on a key issue that troubled him: a split between academic technology and administrative technology. Academic technology reported to the vice president of academic affairs while Brisson oversaw the administrative unit. This split represented a fault line, in Brisson's view. Chief among these pitfalls was the capacity for endless finger-pointing between the two groups. For instance, if problems arose with a computer laboratory, was it the responsibility of the academic support group or the administrative group to step in? Were there redundancies that could be trimmed within a consolidated model? How were financial resources allocated between the two groups? Did they share the same long-term goals and strategies? Brisson eventually managed to consolidate the two units into a common entity reporting to him. He set about melding these segments into a coordinated team dedicated to supporting all IT needs.

His analysis of the university's technical capabilities proved more problematic in a way that resisted a simple resolution. Maryville's computer network was an older one. It did not feature an extensive fiber network. Brisson concluded that the network needed not just a tweak but a transformation. The servers, likewise, were older and in definite need of upgrade. Such physical infrastructure is not what comes to mind for many people regarding IT needs. Yet without proper infrastructure and fiber, cell phones, laptops, and other mobile devices will not operate to their fullest potential.

Brisson recalls that Maryville spent approximately $1 million a year on IT capital investment when he arrived. That sum was not then an insignificant part of the university's budget. But this sum allowed only for incremental updates and patching of existing systems. It simply was insufficient if Maryville was serious about accomplishing its IT goals. A much more ambitious commitment was required.

Lombardi, meanwhile, had plunged into a concerted effort to study technology and determine the potential effect it could have at Maryville. He became convinced that technology was key for the university to boost enrollment and enhance the effectiveness of personalized education and service for all students. He resolved to do whatever it took to leapfrog Maryville at least two or more generations in the technology space.

MARYVILLE'S FIRST-CLASS WIRELESS NETWORK

Brisson remembers a conversation one day when Lombardi asked him what it would take to have a first-class wireless network all over Maryville's West County campus that would place it among the top 10 percent of schools nationwide. A network that would run fast, run all the time, and run without dead spots here and there. Brisson and his team undertook a focused study. A total of $2.5 million a year was the figure that IT determined was necessary. He noted that IT was simply not a "one and done" type of need. A surge for a year or two in IT investment would provide some short-term improvements but not solve the long-term challenges holding the institution back.

Senior leadership and the board of trustees resolved to make such an IT upgrade a top institutional priority. Budget priorities were shifted to free funds. Finding another $1.5 million a year was far from easy. But other priorities were placed on the back burner or discarded as the necessary funding was found. Brisson notes with satisfaction that Maryville has maintained this financial commitment over time and even enhanced it after his retirement from day-to-day involvement in St. Louis (he continues to consult for the university from his Florida residence). Such continual reinvestment now totals more than $5 million per year and has allowed Maryville to become a first-rate institution in terms of IT capability. It has provided the foundation upon which many other technology-related programs have been launched.

Brisson explains that it is actually quite simple: the whole Active Learning Ecosystem (ALE) initiative, as well as other computer-related initiatives such as Maryville's cybersecurity and online academic programs, would have failed without the infrastructure created and subsequently maintained. A university must have tremendous bandwidth and Wi-Fi, along with a highly reliable network throughout campus, for all that to happen. Maryville possesses great bandwidth and connectivity today throughout its campus. There are seldom, if any, dead spots or times when the systems run slowly. Without such great technological infrastructure, people on devices like iPads and smartphones would not be able to utilize them to their full capacity. Frustration would build. Finger-pointing would start. But little of that frustration has occurred at Maryville. In fact, from 2007–2011, the number one frustration students shared in surveys regarded the connectivity of the campus network. From 2012 to today, it ranks third among highest student satisfaction items.

Brisson notes that as a former teacher himself, he is pleased that the conversation about using technology in the classroom shifted to a discussion centered on how well technological innovations would integrate into teaching and learning at Maryville. No one worried whether the technology would function properly. The IT role became one of helping facilitate and implement those academic initiatives while not allowing technical issues and infrastructure shortcomings to stand in the way. Maryville's consistent investment of millions in technological infrastructure had laid the foundation for a transformation of its academic programs and student experience.

UNDERWRITING TECHNOLOGICAL INFRASTRUCTURE

Attorney Tom Boudreau graduated as one of the university's first male students in 1973 with a double major in English and philosophy. He has served on the board of trustees for two decades including twelve years as its chair. Boudreau has obviously seen many changes and alterations to campus and university programming. He credits both the board and senior leadership for getting on the same page regarding the need for substantial, annual technological investment.

Boudreau considers the sums approved by the board to underwrite technological infrastructure as a key component underlying the university's success in boosting enrollment. This trend is demonstrated through Maryville's consistent designation as the second fastest growing private university in the country as tracked by *The Chronicle of Higher Education*. Maryville's enrollment has more than tripled (3,300 to 11,000 students) during the decade stretching from autumn of 2009 through fall of 2020, the period measured by *The Chronicle*. In fact, Maryville's enrollment grew over 10 percent during the height of the global pandemic.

Boudreau says that one of the things he hears again and again, especially from current students and those students who are thinking about enrolling at Maryville, is how powerful and top-notch its wireless system is. Campus visitors and residents take notice and talk favorably about it. When they get on their device, whether it be their cell phone or their laptop or their iPad, they are surprised and pleased by how fast Maryville's systems operate. And it is that way everywhere on its campus. For the generation of students who will attend any university, Maryville's level of connectivity is essential.

Joanne Soliday of Credo contends that the IT infrastructure decision reflects a key trait that distinguishes the university from other institutions: Maryville's ability to focus outside of itself. Unlike most schools, Soliday argues that Maryville faces outward rather than inward. Such inward-facing institutions often do not fix problems because they do not truly understand their surrounding environment. Maryville, on the other hand, looks to push boundaries. Problems are confronted and overcome by searching out best practices prevalent beyond campus and, sometimes, the higher education industry. Such learning is then shared throughout the institution rather than hoarded within a single division.

"Maryville stays at the cutting edge of what technology can do in higher education," Soliday reflects. "Maryville maintains great curiosity because it recognizes that many other fine organizations in various industries did not stay up with technological innovation and perished. Couple that with a desire to comprehend that the next generation of learners—of all ages—come to campus with a different skill set, attitude, and background than ever before. It represents a crucial advantage for the university."

This discussion about Maryville's commitment to invest in and leverage technological infrastructure cannot be understated. The decision to invest in technology—and the willpower to commit to do so consistently over time—made other crucial initiatives possible. It is just another prime example of Maryville sequencing its steps thoughtfully, appropriately, and carefully to allow for subsequent progress on many fronts. Many individuals who mustered the willpower and gathered the funding to underwrite the technological infrastructure and make it a reality will admit they did not fully appreciate all possibilities at the outset. But they recognize in retrospect that without such infrastructure, Maryville's future would be limited and restricted rather than expansive and open to possibility.

LIFE COACHING

Maryville has completely upended the traditional system of student advising found within academe. Its students have more than one advisor, each one possessing different degrees of expertise in varying topics to ensure student success. It has blended elements of student life, academics, and support services into a coherent whole life model called life coaching. This model means that a student is no longer a hostage to the relative availability or engagement of one person but rather has a network of support on which to draw.

Each full-time, traditional undergraduate student is assigned a life coach. That relationship is designed to stretch throughout a student's entire time on campus—and beyond into career support and advice. Maryville believes that this relationship based on one-on-one ongoing interaction increases overall student success rates and satisfaction.

> **Each full-time, traditional undergraduate student is assigned a life coach. That relationship is designed to stretch throughout a student's entire time on campus—and beyond into career support and advice.**

Maryville University's student retention and graduation rates illustrate the success of this model. A decade ago, Maryville's freshman to sophomore retention rate hovered around 72 percent for traditional undergraduates. That figure was comparable to national averages for a school the size and character of Maryville. This rate continues to hover at about the same mark nationwide during the past ten years. The freshman to sophomore retention rate at Maryville, however, recently has approached 90 percent. Maryville's graduation rate is well above the national average at 75 percent and its career placement is close to perfection at 98 percent.

The university has hired more than a dozen life coaches thus far. They represent the diversity of the students at large. Different students have different needs, so possessing a cadre of individuals with varying professional experiences remains desirable compared to a roster of folks with similar backgrounds. There is no single academic major or professional résumé that Maryville seeks when hiring life coaches. The university does not specifically seek licensed counselors for this role. Instead, it looks for candidates who demonstrate an abiding passion for and commitment to student-centeredness.

Life coaches do not work a standard nine-to-five sort of day. Students have concerns that arise throughout the day and night.

Modern technology allows them to convey their concerns at any time. Life coaches must respond as promptly as possible to student needs, whether a weekday or weekend. And issues may also be raised by the parents of those students, who must also receive a satisfactory and prompt response. That type of round-the-clock work schedule and ongoing commitment is obviously not suitable for everyone's lifestyle. That is why Maryville takes such pains to identify candidates who embrace such a relentless pace rather than recoil from it.

Maryville expects to ramp up the number of life coaches as its traditional undergraduate enrollment grows. The university will closely assess the number life coaches to keep its student to life coach ratio low. It wants to ensure that life coaches have a reasonable and meaningful opportunity to establish a close relationship with each student. A life coach remains assigned to the same student for all four years. Their interaction with their student starts even before they set foot on campus.

Vice President of Student Success Jennifer McCluskey supervises the life coaches. A respected member of the university staff for nearly two decades, McCluskey's first role was as director of retention initiatives within the enrollment department started in 2002. Six years later, she became associate vice president of academic affairs and worked closely with faculty in developing the first-year experience. That role led to her current position overseeing the life coaches as well as career services, international student success, study abroad, disability student support, and the university library. This represents a new and comprehensive division that is absolutely essential to a student's success.

McCluskey explains how the life coaching process typically unfolds at Maryville:

Once students indicate that Maryville University is the place they wish to attend, each one is assigned a life coach. In the months before orientation, their assigned life coach reaches out to introduce themselves, establish contact, and begin to form a working relationship. The life coach electronically sends each student multiple diagnostic instruments to review, complete, and send back. The results from those diagnostic tools are then analyzed and compiled into a student profile. This profile helps the life coach understand factors such as how a particular student best learns, their relative strengths and weaknesses, and their personality traits. These results are, in turn, shared with the student so each party can begin to recognize relative skills and shortcomings. They can begin to formulate goals and strategies that might prove most effective.

These profiles are also shared with faculty members so they can begin to assess the learning styles and needs of their new students before these individuals even reach their classroom. This is the key to personalized learning within an Active Learning Ecosystem. Former Vice President of Academic Affairs Finch reports that she has heard various groups of faculty talking about the life coaching program and the excitement they feel about working in collaboration with the life coaches. Being able to get background information about their students in advance is something they consider beneficial for all concerned. The degree of collaboration between life coaches and faculty members remains a work in progress. It varies based on circumstances and personalities. But thoughtful and collaborative teamwork between the life coach and faculty member has proved essential when life coaching achieves peak effectiveness.

The first two years on campus for a traditional undergraduate student are spent predominantly working one-on-one with their life coach. Students learn to adjust to college life, develop effective study habits, navigate the general curriculum, discover the variety of campus offices available, explore extracurricular opportunities, and evaluate various majors.

This comprehensive support is especially important as first-year students become sophomores. This transition normally proves the most crucial from a retention standpoint because most departing students leave after their first year. If a student stays for their second year, the vast majority will advance through graduation. Typically, about 20–25 percent of Maryville students will decide to change their major during their first two years. Before life coaches, they would have shuttled between faculty members as their advisors based on their major. Now, each student enjoys the stability and continuity of working with a single life coach who connects students to various faculty in different departments.

As their junior year approaches, each student selects a faculty mentor from within their major(s). This faculty mentor helps counsel the student regarding course options and selection, especially within the major; experiential opportunities such as internships; and career options typically pursued by departmental students. Together, the life coach and faculty member work to complement the expertise and training of the other to mentor a student. This partnership also allows the faculty member to concentrate the bulk of their engagement within the realm of academics, where they are typically most comfortable and possess the greatest degree of expertise.

EXCEPTIONAL STUDENT SUPPORT = STUDENT SUCCESS

Coaches and faculty alike receive favorable feedback attesting to the merits of this relatively new experiment. Associate Professor Steve Coxon of the School of Education recalls a vivid example when he was out in the community at a medical facility having blood drawn. A woman saw his insurance card, recognized his connection with Maryville, and spoke enthusiastically about her eighteen-year-old daughter who was enrolled there. This mother was delighted that her daughter was able to benefit from all the extra support and assistance that she received from her life coach. Coxon says he has heard the same from many others as well, although he fortunately did "not have to give blood in all those cases."

Julie Krebel graduated from Maryville in 2011 with a double major in psychology and sociology. She then spent two years in graduate school at Illinois State University, where she made a final decision to pursue a career in higher education. After earning her master's degree, Krebel returned to her alma mater, first working in the admissions department and then as a life coach.

Krebel describes this professional role as a lot like being a parent without the bills! This perspective leads one to begin to understand the sense of elation and gratification she derives from her work. She sees how much each student changes, opens up, and tries new things as she works with them. That process continually amazes her. A key factor is the discovery over time of the nuances of each student. Thus, she might work with Sara a little differently than she works with Joshua. She really taps into how each student learns best or how they can be pushed to learn in a new, better way. Life coaching has proved a natural and rewarding fit for her. She really loved her Maryville experiences as a student and now derives the similar satisfaction from helping current students explore and discover their own personalized path.

Corey Baker is another Maryville alum who has served within the ranks of its administration. He graduated in 2007 with a degree in organizational leadership. The remarks he delivered as the student commencement speaker that year remain a lifelong highlight. Baker describes other beneficial effects that the life coaching program has introduced at the university. The university has demonstrated the value of its personalized education in its recruitment efforts by highlighting the life coaching program. It proves that Maryville believes in one-on-one attention through designating a specific contact person for each student's ongoing questions or concerns. In addition, students also benefit from the tutelage of faculty mentors who now concentrate primarily on their specialty: academics. This one-two tandem of life coach and faculty member

> **This one-two tandem of life coach and faculty member provides an extremely strong support mechanism for students.**

provides an extremely strong support mechanism for students. Life coaching has proved an easy sell in enrollment. It clearly demonstrates that the university invests in each student's potential while making their success a top priority.

ACTIVE LEARNING ECOSYSTEM

"Absolutely the most student-centered approach to learning" is how President Lombardi describes the underlying philosophy of the Active Learning Ecosystem (ALE) initiative that the university instituted in the fall of 2015. He contends that by the middle of this decade, most, if not all, universities will utilize such technology-based approaches in their teaching and learning methods. The pandemic has certainly accelerated that transition.

This approach importantly allows students to learn differently within the same academic space. Individuals can tailor their study methods according to their strengths and comprehend information in the most effective and efficient way. It represents the farthest thing from a one-size-fits-all approach to teaching and learning that has been so common throughout higher education for well over a century. The ALE gives Maryville students the chance to personalize their education preferences while functioning within an enhanced technology environment.

Part of the ALE is a university program known as Digital World. Maryville has earned recognition twice since 2016 as an Apple Distinguished School by Apple Inc. because of its Digital World initiative. This designation is coveted and given by Apple solely to those educational institutions that meet criteria for innovation, leadership, and educational excellence while demonstrating a clear vision in executing exemplary learning environments. Maryville was the only higher education institution to earn this distinction in 2016 and now is the only university to earn it twice (2018).

All traditional, full-time undergraduate students and graduate students from select programs are given an iPad to utilize throughout their course of studies. The iPad is free and theirs to keep, maintain, and utilize to personalize their academic experience. It is loaded with more than 150 learning apps and contains digital access to all course materials as part of Maryville's partnership with Red Shelf.

Full-time faculty, as well as designated adjuncts and staff members, receive iPads as well. That system means that Maryville has purchased and placed 5,500 of these devices into circulation. Those figures make the university's initiative the largest such one at a private university in the nation. Keep in mind the following facts as perspective: the iPad was first released in 2010, less than a decade ago; in the year 2000, nearly two decades ago, only half of all US households even had a computer of some kind.

Maryville's cost to distribute iPads thus far has totaled more than $2 million. During this deployment, Maryville has not raised tuition nor fees for its students. Rather this money was defrayed through operating surpluses. A further illustration of Maryville's prudent fiscal management.

ALE investments did not end there. Besides the annual cost of providing devices to new students each year, the university hired a director of learning technology and support. In this role, Sam Harris (one of five Apple Distinguished Educators at Maryville) manages the day-to-day and sees to the nuts and bolts. He provides many types of support, including a wide array of technology workshops. Harris has helped organize student support groups so that technologically savvy individuals can assist peers who might lag behind. At the same time, Harris has witnessed a dramatic increase in the use of lecture capture software. This software allows faculty to record their lectures. Students can watch them before they come to class. This innovation allows classroom time to be spent on hands-on, active learning rather than passive listening. Such techniques have proven especially popular in the health professions and sciences.

The university surmised early on that ALE would only be successful if faculty embraced technology along with students and within the classroom. In order to do so, faculty would need ongoing training to appreciate all iPad applications—and how to utilize them effectively with students who might know as much if not more about the technology than the professor.

Maryville's remedy? Extend annual faculty contracts by two weeks. At a cost of nearly $500,000 annually, a week of training is provided in the spring and another in the fall. These sessions are offered on campus and led by the Finch Center for Teaching and Learning, which is faculty designed and managed. Sessions cover diverse topics such as introducing available apps, sharing classroom experiences, brain development and learning theory, discussing best practices, and offering tips to develop creative and engaging content. Sharing this information has facilitated valuable information exchange among Maryville's four academic schools.

Jesse Kavadlo has taught at Maryville for more than a decade. Like many faculty members at the university, he wears two hats: professor of English and as director of the Center for Teaching and Learning. In his director role, he helps conduct the two weeklong training sessions. Kavadlo has realized there is no single way to do the training or convince faculty to embrace the technology. Instead, he works with them individually and gradually to discover ways to enhance utilization of the iPad. Kavadlo also notes that the university provides ninety-minute training sessions every other week for a full semester. He emphasizes that, "It is crucial for faculty to consider technology as a way to enhance teaching and learning outcomes and not just as a piece of fancy equipment. Put another way, faculty must view the iPad as a means to an end and not as the end result itself."

What about Kavadlo's personal experiences using the iPad in his own classes? He has found that he uses the iPad much more in the classroom over time. One easy way to make a classroom more student-centered is by incorporating aspects of technology—say electronic examples of student writing or a video clip or an audio clip. He no longer has to stand alone in front of the room. He remains physically within a circle surrounded by students and pulls examples up using the iPad. But because the students have the same technology, Kavadlo can ask them to join him. Because of the iPad, he has been able to assign students all sorts of multimedia or multimodal projects throughout the semester that can be shared. These types of assignments demonstrate that students comprehend the material as demonstrated through examination of their essays or other projects. Their mastery may even be revealed through some sort of emerging mapping, storyboarding, and/or script writing techniques. The technology allows students to become much more invested in demonstrating what is important to them and what they have learned. Many times, Kavadlo has been pleased to witness a student who struggles initially put together an excellent shared product by the end of a semester.

ALE has also enabled the classroom to move beyond traditional four-wall parameters to venues that can vary from class to class, week to week. Kyra Krakos, associate professor of biology, notes that "the initiative has allowed the university's sustainability courses to be taught in an engaging way. Digital World has moved the university to the point where classrooms exist outside of and/or beyond the physical classroom," Krakos points out. "In Sustainability 150, for example, classes in thirteen of the fifteen weeks of the semester are held off campus within the greater St. Louis metropolitan area. That type of experience would simply not have been possible before the iPads and Digital World. Likewise, in upper-division science classes, ALE allows for real-time data collection in the field. Classes can analyze what they collect on-site using their iPads. That type of experience provides a new type of laboratory—doing real science in real time in the real world. That kind of field science had proved transformative for students," she contends.

What kind of report card have these various teaching and learning techniques earned among the Maryville community? According to Sam Harris, surveys indicate an overall 97 percent favorability rating.

Nearly all faculty have been trained to use technology. And while faculty are not required to use the iPads in their classrooms, more than 90 percent acknowledge doing so. Nearly half indicate they have incorporated the device into all of their courses. By utilizing technology in the classroom, Maryville prepares students for what they will experience in the professional world. The university creates spaces for students to experiment and prepare themselves for what will come next in their professional lives.

A "CULTURE OF NO FEAR"

Assistant Professor Dustin York has served for six years as director of the undergraduate and graduate communications programs at the university. York cites a "culture of no fear" as the main reason why he has enjoyed his tenure at the university so much. Experimentation is encouraged while it is understood that with progress comes some failures. He points to that culture as the lifeblood of why Maryville's faculty, staff, and students have maintained their confidence despite venturing beyond their comfort zones and innovating.

> York cites a "culture of no fear" as the main reason why he has enjoyed his tenure at the university so much. Experimentation is encouraged while it is understood that with progress comes some failures.

That environment has allowed York to take a leadership role in shaping how academic progress occurs within the classroom at the university. It helps to account for why so many of his academic colleagues mention his name first when asked to provide an example of a Maryville faculty member who continually innovates. York admits that each semester he purposely formulates a technological project for his classes in an area in which he lacks expertise. That way, he and his students can learn together and teach one another.

York's work in introducing innovations to his instruction techniques emanates from a fundamental belief that learning occurs more readily outside the classroom than within. That belief helps explain the premium he places regarding students pursuing learning opportunities within the wider community. Many of these experiences, for example, might allow a student to earn a certificate demonstrating their facility with a cutting-edge tool such as Salesforce. Such certificates underscore that a student is up to date in their understanding of technology and supplements their Maryville academic credentials. They might even lead to an employment opportunity.

York remains a proponent of the flipped classroom model. Reading assignments and lecture materials are formulated, recorded, and uploaded for easy access in advance of classroom sessions. Students are expected to read and be familiar with these materials before they come to class. When they arrive, they encounter a physical classroom configuration where the professor sits among the students to facilitate interaction. What ensues during the classroom session is an initial but brief conversation about the readings and/or lectures designed to make sure everyone has completed their assignments and is literally and figuratively on the same page. Once York is convinced that is the case, students will break into huddle groups to explore case studies, undertake projects, or formulate presentations for their peers. On occasion, classes will be held offsite at local corporations. The iPads that all Maryville students possess allow the group access to any pertinent information wherever they may be physically located. Thus, the sharing of information and interaction is assured. The same goes for utilization of the many apps that the university provides to its students. York notes that the playing field for all students is leveled in these ways as no one possesses an inherent advantage over others. York challenges all his students to develop a multifaceted mix of skills demonstrating facility in writing, speaking, researching, and using various technologies. Their education is therefore well rounded and comprehensive, preparing them for a range of possibilities rather than a singular focus or employment opportunity.

Students are strongly encouraged to compile all their academic work in one online space. By the time they are seniors, most, if not all, students possess a personal website constructed to showcase their abilities for graduate school admission officers, corporate employers, or community leaders—an increasing number of whom rank among the alumni of his programs. York feels these websites represent a leg up for many Maryville students. In this way, besides a diploma, a student can demonstrate their expertise with challenging work. This factor may differentiate them from graduates of other institutions who possess a diploma but cannot readily showcase work projects they have completed.

York is not a big believer in utilizing a few major exams during the semester to evaluate student achievement. He prefers continual review of ongoing assignments and projects to ensure students keep up and master them. He feels that faculty should want students to retain information while in class, immediately after they complete the class, and for an extended time stretching as long as ten to twenty years out. In other words, student evaluations should not be "gotcha" moments where evaluators seek to produce a range of grades within a class, York contends. Rather, they should monitor a student's progress continually throughout a semester so their mastery of subject matter is demonstrated over many varied assignments.

York has not found a great difference when instructing in-person versus online courses. The biggest one, in his view, is that online courses extend for just eight weeks compared to sixteen weeks in traditional in-person classes. Thus, he feels the online courses may demand greater academic rigor because of time compression. York emphasizes, though, that the underlying academic approach and learning outcomes remain the same regardless of format. Assignments and evaluations remain identical.

When asked how he keeps up with the myriad of technological innovations influencing modern communications, his mastery is possible because he is a self-proclaimed nerd. He feels that all professors are, to one extent or another, nerds in one way or another. York admits he actually enjoys the process of trying to absorb the impact of emerging trends and technologies. He loves to discover what innovations succeed and which fail—and the reasons underlying these results. York claims it is empowering to stay abreast of the constant ebbs and flows of one's field. He tries to impart this enthusiasm for lifelong learning to his students and readily acknowledges what he has learned from them.

THE USE OF ARTIFICIAL INTELLIGENCE

Artificial intelligence is a topic that currently intrigues York the most. It is defined as the theory and development of computer systems able to perform tasks that customarily require human intelligence such as visual perception, speech recognition, and ability to make decisions or translate between languages. York believes it is a powerful tool that will quickly improve and introduce many enhancements in society and within academia. York contends it will eventually allow any user to find information, personalize that information, and benefit from a compilation of information that continually grows over time. He likens the potential reach of artificial intelligence to Google, which expands its knowledge base every time someone conducts a search.

There are specific benefits of artificial intelligence that York foresees for academic interactions. Artificial intelligence will enhance the ability of students to discover, research, and review pertinent information about a topic before they come to class. The greatest benefit for students that York visualizes, however, is the ability for artificial intelligence to pinpoint the areas where a student has sufficiently mastered information and where they have gaps. It will then probe those areas of weakness to provide more assistance and develop quiz questions the student can employ to ensure they have plugged those gaps before moving further in their studies. It will further personalize the process by helping students discover where they most need help.

"Artificial intelligence remains in its infancy concerning most classroom applications," according to York. A base level known as chat bots are becoming increasingly widespread. Some of his classes have developed them during a semester. These function much like Siri where simple questions are posed and answered. The next step will be customizing and personalizing information to facilitate individual interaction. That interaction will require a conversation of sorts where artificial intelligence provides specific personal recommendations.

ADAPTIVE LEARNING IN ACTION

Adaptive learning is another issue that intrigues York based on its potential. This term utilizes computer algorithms to orchestrate the interaction with the learner. It analyzes a wide variety of tools, information, and techniques available at any one time to teach a student in the best possible way. Adaptive learning employs aspects of computer science, artificial intelligence, psychology, and brain science as it scans and pinpoints learning experiences that are able to most benefit each learner based on their circumstances and characteristics. One hypo-thetical example that York provides might pertain to an online student who has a long commute to work and has demonstrated a facility for audio learning. Under adaptive learning, video lectures might be converted into audio podcasts for such a student to utilize during a long commute. This student might lack the time and circumstances to watch an extended video, so why not convert the material into another format they can consume more readily? York notes it is the same information and material but packaged and provided to each student in a way that is most effective for their learning modality.

York recognizes that many of these terms and technologies can breed fear among those who hear them and are not familiar with them yet. He urges the fearful not to get hung up on the terminology and technologies. In his view, all these technologies and techniques can, when boiled down to their essence, be classified simply as effective customer service—the type that traditional retail establishments like Nordstrom have provided to their customers for decades. These new techniques and technologies will prove effective only if they facilitate getting to know each individual and providing them with personal-ized solutions best suited to their needs. And such great customer service and experiences, he believes, will be demanded increasingly by students and parents as they seek out the best academic institution for their given circumstances and needs. In some ways, this philosophy demonstrates that much has changed in the academic environment. In other ways, it also reveals that the underlying fundamentals of helping humans achieve their goals has remained much the same.

ALE increasingly differentiates Maryville from other institutions. It has also provided an ancillary but vital benefit: it has leveled the playing field within the classroom. Faculty utilize the same device as students. Students all possess the same device. Previously, one student might possess a high-end laptop computer costing thousands while another student had to make do with paper and pen. This imbalance based on varying socio-economic circumstances often adversely impacted students of color or those who were economically disadvantaged. It was difficult if not impossible to quantify the effects of such technological imbalances. Now, such imbalances are eradicated. The talent, toil, and tenacity of the student serve as the primary determining factors for academic success under ALE. This represents a vital step in the democratization of higher education.

> ALE increasingly differentiates Maryville from other institutions. It has also provided an ancillary but vital benefit: it has leveled the playing field within the classroom. Faculty utilize the same device as students. Students all possess the same device.

Nearly one student out of every five surveyed indicated ALE served as a major factor convincing them to enroll at Maryville. Enrollment counselors emphasize to families that the program is not a gimmick whereby a student is handed an iPad and wished good luck. The device instead becomes an integral part of their daily life and educational experiences. There is no hidden or additional cost to the student or their family for the device or the training needed to utilize it effectively. It promotes digital literacy and encourages students to become well-educated citizens of an emerging technological world.

ONLINE EDUCATION

A campus task force from several divisions, under then Vice President of Enrollment Miller, was appointed to study online education and make a recommendation regarding its viability during the spring semester of

2010. This task force's original inclination was to examine only online classes that might be utilized to allow a student to fulfill their academic requirements through a mix of traditional and in-classroom instruction, complemented by some additional designated online offerings.

The task force met only a few times. It quickly reached a conclusion reflecting keen self-awareness: Maryville possessed neither the expertise nor the resources to move into or ramp up quickly in the online world. The task force thus made a recommendation to the president to explore forming a partnership with a respected firm already knowledgeable and experienced in the field. This alliance, it was felt, would best provide the bedrock required to determine how and where to move into online education. The task force also mandated that any online experiences at the university would, first and foremost, need to preserve the same educational integrity and high academic standards as traditional offerings.

The evaluative process of potential partners began in the summer and continued through the fall of 2010. The process was not without its challenges. Maryville, after much research and consultation with other institutions, formulated a list of potential partner firms. Vice President Miller recalls that Maryville approached several different companies. All but one of these firms turned Maryville down.

Only one company—Compass Knowledge Group, based in Florida—considered Maryville a potentially viable online partner. This modest arrangement would have involved Compass Knowledge Group marketing a few online courses that Maryville faculty and staff would develop.

Just when it seemed a signed contract between the two entities appeared likely, an unexpected wrinkle emerged. Another company with significant online experience and expertise, Embanet, purchased Compass Knowledge Group. There was a downside to that transaction from Maryville's perspective. Embanet had previously turned down the opportunity to form an online alliance with the university. It was nerve-racking for Maryville to know that one of the companies that had already turned it down had purchased the only company expressing interest in forming a partnership.

However, the two Compass Knowledge Group executives who had visited Maryville continued to champion a partnership after the merger. The final decision came down to a vote by a transition team composed of individuals from the two merged firms, now consolidated into a new company called Embanet-Compass Knowledge Group. One vote tipped the balance in favor of Maryville.

"That is how close Maryville came to not moving ahead into the online realm," Miller remembers. Needless to say, everyone on campus was waiting on pins and needles for the phone call to see how the vote had gone. Fortunately, it was good news. Soon the partner company became known just as Embanet. Then Embanet was purchased by Pearson, a British-owned global leader in higher education marketing and major player in the online field. This change marked an accelerated change in the Maryville online programs. To think about where Maryville stands now with its online programs and to know how close the university was to being denied the chance to get started simply continues to amaze Miller.

An MSN nursing program in an online format started in the fall of 2011. It had taken approximately eighteen months to make it happen, start to finish. Maryville's nursing faculty designed the program according to state and national professional standards, and Pearson provided marketing and admission support. Maryville correctly surmised that if it could deliver a high-quality nursing program that the nursing profession certified as outstanding, then in the future, it could deliver other programs at a high-quality level.

This partnership was and continues to be an outstanding success. Initial estimates were that Maryville would have four hundred MSN students enrolled at its peak. In 2019 Maryville has more than 2,700 MSN students from forty-seven states enrolled.

Maryville decided at the outset of its partnership with Pearson that the admission requirements for any online program would be the same as for a traditional, classroom-based one. That standard of consistency has never wavered. All populations—whether traditional undergraduate, online undergraduate, traditional graduate, online graduate—must meet the same specific admission requirements required of a given program. No quality adjustments would occur, nor would leeway be given when Maryville introduced online programs. That step assured the same high standard of quality among students whether in a physical or virtual classroom. A similar step was taken regarding the hiring of highly credentialed faculty to deliver online programs.

This initial success led to a more comprehensive partnership with Pearson. Maryville now offers more than forty online degree programs at the undergraduate and graduate levels across all of its schools. This effort serves 7,500 working adults across fifty states, and it grows at a rate of 18–22 percent per year.

In higher education, it often takes years to create new classes or degree programs. Maryville is cutting that time down to months.

Associate Academic Vice President Tammy Gocial has enjoyed two different employment stints at Maryville, including the last decade in her current position. She contends that the "move to pursue and introduce online education represents a watershed decision in the university's history." Online education, for sure, was a crucial step for Maryville, she notes. It was also a challenging one. There were a lot of skeptics among the faculty who were not sure what the online experience would entail. Could Maryville offer good quality education in an online format? Maryville has emphatically proven that it can, in her view. The decision to go online was extremely important because it opened up Maryville's enrollment to students from throughout the whole country and on an international level. The university has been able to capitalize on that opportunity and now also offers many great programs in the online world that complement, rather than compete with, in-person programs.

The growth in the online programs, both working in partnership with Pearson and in other instances on its own, has generated substantial net revenue and diversified Maryville's revenue streams. Their success required some institutional structural changes. The enrollment department divided in two, as noted earlier. Miller maintained oversight of the traditional undergraduate population, the Student Service Center, and international recruitment.

Another division formed to concentrate on adult and online undergraduate and graduate programs. Dan Viele joined the staff in June of 2013 to create this brand-new programming model as the first dean of Maryville's School of Adult and Online Education. It should be emphasized he did not inherit an established division but needed to create it from scratch.

Viele possessed an interesting background with varied career experiences. First arriving in St. Louis in 1990 from his native central Illinois, he lived only about five minutes from the West County campus for nearly a quarter century. Viele familiarized himself with Maryville at arm's length, noting its traditional focus on programs in the health professions and business while earning tenure as a professor of accounting at another institution.

Viele would serve at three other higher education institutions before coming to Maryville, his academic career interrupted once by an eight-year stint working in Silicon Valley. While contemplating retirement, Viele got a call from President Lombardi at Maryville and was impressed with his vision for online education. Viele looks back and contends he had so much fun being present at the creation.

"The thing that most uniquely describes Maryville University today is its strategic vision for what higher education ought to be," Viele says. The institutional culture is one where the university acts nimbly, flexibly, and remains market relevant. Maryville focuses on serving its students—whether it is lifelong learning or career choices—to offer what employers and organizations look for. That market relevance is crucial and represents a good return on investment.

There are several factors that Viele cites as crucial to ensuring successful online education. The process starts with a keen understanding of the needs of online students, who are generally adult learners leading busy lives without much free time; they must balance many competing priorities vying for their attention. Convenience, flexibility, cost, and time to completion of a degree remain paramount online student concerns.

Viele points to Maryville's commitment to take online education a step further by removing all physical barriers to access and promoting greater flexibility in scheduling. This format opened up an entirely new academic world divorced from the confines of physical space. One method of instruction did not replace or supplant the other. Instead, each complemented the other. Success can only be achieved in online education at a university, Viele contends, by establishing such an equilibrium.

There are important distinctions to highlight when understanding how content is delivered in an online format and how classroom interaction transpires within that academic sphere. The online format, in actuality, provides for certain teaching methods that are sometimes more limited in a traditional classroom space. It offers an excellent chance for what has become known as active learning, or flipping the classroom. It is centered in a belief that many students will learn better by doing rather than by listening. While such active learning teaching methods are not limited strictly to the online arena and are practiced increasingly in traditional classrooms, active learning has remained a prominent and dominant feature of online instruction.

CAPTURING THE CONTENT

Maryville has invested significantly in sophisticated ways to capture and package the content that is shared in flipped classrooms. The university has hired a team of technical people who work in partnership with faculty to take traditional course content and translate it to an online format. Faculty maintain their role as the lead content experts. But the designers play a crucial role assisting in this scenario. They may employ cutting-edge video production. They may build simulations that illustrate concepts. They may include authoritative information available through websites or libraries located elsewhere throughout the world. In many cases, they have used this sophisticated assistance to enhance the information presented in their traditional classrooms as well.

Maryville created two on-campus studios to help produce such online course content. The role of the faculty member within the online format tends to shift significantly from that of a lecturer to that of an engager. Classroom discussions shift as well. Instead of just a few hours of face-to-face time within a given week, discussions taking place in an online class may occur over a period of several days and be ongoing, robust, and round-the-clock. Viele believes strongly from personal experience that it is much harder for a student to hide in an online class than in a physical classroom. Online students must demonstrate their mastery of subject material before advancing to the next hurdle. Faculty preparing to teach in an online format must be prepared for differences in format and technique. They must be ready to focus primarily on student engagement rather than on lecturing.

Viele admits that Maryville's success in the online world is far from a personal accomplishment. He first salutes the technical staff that packages the content in such an engaging, interesting manner for student consumption. He commends the faculty for their subject expertise and their willingness to keep an open mind and convey that knowledge through alternative delivery mechanisms.

Viele points to four major groups at Maryville that he believes have derived tangible benefits from the online format: students, faculty, administration, and corporate partners. As just one example, some faculty have admitted that they have discovered certain teaching techniques through their online classrooms that will enhance the learning taking place within their traditional classrooms.

Maryville's presence on a national and global scale has now expanded significantly because it is no longer confined by its geographic location. Its financial standing has been strengthened by the incorporation of new student audiences that have complemented—rather than cannibalized—its traditional, classroom-based academic programs. Its partnership with Pearson has introduced new instructional offerings and brought its marketing expertise to the table. Substantial investment in staff and facilities has boosted internal capabilities and resources to deliver improved instructional techniques and programming. Cost structures for all the online programs vary from traditional programs and are clearly outlined through a homepage link on the university's website. Viele admits that it has become very satisfying to know that online education has positively affected almost every dimension of the university.

> **Online education has positively affected almost every dimension of the university.**

CYBERSECURITY

The story regarding the emergence and evolution of a cybersecurity program at the university is noteworthy. Graduates pursue careers across a variety of industries to secure, defend, and investigate information systems and networks. This field had remained largely in the background of the information industry for years with relatively few individuals devoting significant focus to it. Then a series of highly publicized international incidents such as the Edward Snowden case; the Julian Assange imbroglio; data breaches at large corporations such as Target, Capital One, and others; as well as accusations of Russian meddling in the 2016 US presidential election shone the spotlight on it. Such awareness created huge demand for trained professionals.

As is typical at Maryville, the institution did not suffer from paralysis by analysis. It moved quickly, nimbly, and with intense focus to create a new academic program. After just sixty days, an advisory board of respected industry professionals had joined with Maryville faculty to map out quality undergraduate and graduate programs that could be taught in traditional physical classrooms as well as online.

Within eighteen months of the introduction of these programs, more than five hundred Maryville students pursued undergraduate and graduate degrees in cybersecurity. That number has continued to climb. The Maryville University Cyber Fusion Center (CFC) has been established as an innovative student-run and faculty-managed security operations center. The center is designed to provide a wide range of cost-free services to nonprofit organizations, charities, schools, and small businesses, which, in turn, allow students real-world internship opportunities to apply what they are learning. The CFC monitors various data feeds from around the globe and then integrates these analytics into actionable intelligence. Students obtain academic credit for their work in the CFC.

The CFC conjures up images of Star Wars. The dynamism of its tracking operations captures one's attention and makes one aware of the many challenges and dangers that lurk around the clock and around the world. CFC demonstrates there are no breaks, pauses, or vacations in this field. Activity is a constant, as is the need for top-notch, engaged, and motivated professionals.

All cybersecurity activities are conceived to meet Maryville students where they are at. The cybersecurity job market has a negative 4 percent unemployment rate. Therefore, Maryville's skill-fully trained and educated students are in high demand for jobs commanding starting salaries ranging from $75,000–$90,000. In most cases, students are placed in jobs well before commencement so they can hit the ground running the day after if they so choose.

AN EXCEPTIONAL ALUMNA SUCCESS STORY— SUSANNE MAGEE

Susanne Magee is a 1996 Maryville graduate. Magee had returned to school as an adult student with two years of course credits under her belt. Many of her basic requirements were already satisfied when she enrolled, so she had the opportunity to explore different majors. She first pursued music therapy. But Magee later learned about other academic opportunities available while exploring the possibilities within a communications major. She decided to pursue that course of study.

The communications major included a speech requirement, which proved beneficial to her personal development by developing confidence in her presentation skills. It also mandated that she complete a computer lab. Magee soon found, to her delight, that she loved computers. She resolved to find a career that would combine her two interests. That career would eventually emerge in the field of cybersecurity, where she has founded two different companies.

Magee developed an interest in protecting information early in her computer career after entering the workforce upon completing her degree. But her two supervisors at the computer company where she worked discouraged her interest in security. "Nobody knows what that is" is the way they explained their inclination to remain aloof from that area. She resolved, therefore, that she would leave that firm and start her own security firm called Tech Card Security. It continues to flourish today with local headquarters in St. Louis. The creation of another cybersecurity firm would follow.

Because of Magee's ties to Maryville and professional expertise, she was asked to join the cybersecurity advisory board. In that role, she offered her opinions regarding what courses should become part of the curriculum, how students could be engaged in internships, and how Maryville could engage with the business sector to provide meaningful job opportunities to graduates of the fledgling program.

She notes the variety of issues that one must be prepared to deal with in the cybersecurity field. Those issues have changed over time. Cybersecurity, in her view, started out just as network security that required actions like putting up a firewall or introducing an antivirus software program. She has since seen giant pivots and shifts to the point where the field stands today. Magee contends that people, especially young ones, are too trusting and share far too much information on Facebook and elsewhere that creates security vulnerabilities. Thus, her firms have more than fifty patents approved or pending around the world to address such weaknesses.

A positive development she has witnessed is that people have increasingly become aware and wary of the dangers posed by tens of millions of unique threats coming from IP addresses that attack critical infrastructures. This scenario offers a wide range of excellent employment opportunities for Maryville graduates in the security field.

Magee notes that Maryville has intentionally focused on encouraging diversity in the field as well as within the university. Cybersecurity has not traditionally been a field where women and minorities have been well represented. But there has been outreach to women and minorities at Maryville, which have helped businesses like hers diversify and become stronger.

Magee also sees demand for individuals who possess additional skills within the field of cybersecurity. In particular, she notes an emerging need for good actuarial people trained in programs such as the one offered at Maryville. These actuaries will be called upon to ascertain and assess the overall risk of cyberattacks and the actuarial tables quantifying such risk. She sees a blending of skill sets within the industry as it matures, evolves, and adapts. Magee salutes Maryville's vision and commitment to provide educational opportunities and reach new audiences through online programs as well as targeted instruction in emerging fields such as cybersecurity.

RAWLINGS SPORT BUSINESS PROGRAM

Another noteworthy Maryville University partnership contains elements of community, academics, and sponsorship all wrapped into one. Formally known as the Rawlings Sport Business Management Program, this partnership resides within Maryville's John E. Simon School of Business. The use of the word "resides" is apt. Rawlings Sporting Goods has maintained its corporate headquarters for more than a decade in Maryville Center, located adjacent to campus on land once owned by the university. The Rawlings logo looms, in fact, on the side of their headquarters, located approximately the length of a football field from the Saints baseball diamond, Weber Field. Such proximity to Weber Field is fitting since Rawlings specializes in producing baseball equipment. When the company moved to West County at the end of 2005, Rawlings told the *St. Louis Business Journal* that the possibility for strategic partnerships with the university was a prime motivation behind its new location.

The company's greatest fame has derived from the production of baseball gloves. It began supplying gloves to the hometown Cardinals in 1906. Designs evolved over time, and Rawlings became the preferred glove of most professional baseball players, a distinction it maintains to the present day. Within the last decade, Rawlings has also diversified its products to include tent canopies, grills, coolers, and chairs. Some of these items are produced under a multiyear deal the firm signed with the National Football League. Thus, its long tradition of commercial success, product innovation, loyalty to the St. Louis community, and being a neighbor to the university qualified it as an ideal corporate partner for Maryville. Rawlings, in fact, contacted the Maryville athletic department soon after its relocation and asked whether Maryville athletes would help test their equipment. Student-athletes offered their feedback.

Pam Horwitz, the retired dean of the John E. Simon School of Business credits Kathy Quinn, the former dean of students, with first raising the concept of establishing a sport business program. Quinn had once taught some business courses at her alma mater. Because at the time the student body skewed heavily female when Rawlings relocated to West County, the university sought academic offerings that might attract greater numbers of male students. Quinn contended that such a sport business program might prove attractive to male students. There were few sport business programs at colleges and universities at that time. The majority of them were housed within departments of education at colleges and universities and focused on providing coaching instruction. Horwitz and Quinn instead had in mind a business degree within the Simon School.

Horwitz trekked across Maryville's campus to Rawlings's head-quarters one day to explore the possibility of a sport business program. She met with Rawlings executives, including Art Chou, who today serves as an adjunct instructor in the program. There was mutual recognition that sport is a multibillion-dollar industry. The sports industry requires product development, pricing strategy, sponsorships, promotions, and marketing. All these facets require sound training in basic business principles combined with specific knowledge of the sports industry. Thus, it seemed a natural progression for the John E. Simon School of Business to offer such a program. Quinn served as its first part-time faculty member.

SUCCESS STORY—JASON WILLIAMS

Robust enrollment ensued. It became apparent to all observers that Maryville had found a gem. But success required broadening the scope of the program and hiring its first full-time head. That individual subsequently appeared on campus in the person of Jason Williams, a personable ex-linebacker who had played football collegiately at New Jersey's Montclair State. Horwitz notes that Williams was an unusual candidate for the job because his background had not been in education or the classroom. The Maryville opportunity, in fact, had been pointed out to him by a mentor who planted the idea of Williams becoming a professor. Williams admits he had never considered such a role before. He mulled over what such a career change would mean. His background had been focused more recently within the marketing and ticketing office of Boston College. His opportunities to instruct and mentor students had been limited. Nonetheless, his professional presence has proved to be a perfect fit during the past decade that he has spent building, leading, and growing the program while at the same time earning a doctorate.

Williams embraced the business of sport concept, recognized its potential, and cultivated great relationships within the sports community, Horwitz contends. Williams made it a model program because he did not simply establish internships for students—he went well beyond that and formulated shared events, encouraged students to do hands-on product research for organizations, and promoted professional development. To use a sports term, the program became win-win for our university, our students, and the organizations they serve.

Rawlings took favorable notice of the program. It appreciated its nurturing of trained students who view sports from a business perspective. All students must complete a menu of fundamental courses in accounting, economics, finance, and communications. This coursework is supplemented by various offerings in sales, traditional and digital marketing, promotions, sponsorships, data analytics, event management, social media, and legal issues. Combine that comprehensive academic package with hands-on work experience gleaned through volunteer and internship opportunities, and firms like Rawlings quickly recognized they benefit immensely from the contributions of trained, motivated students eager to pursue a career in the industry.

CREATION OF THE SPORT BUSINESS MANAGEMENT PROGRAM

In January of 2013, in a press conference at Busch Stadium in downtown St. Louis, Rawlings and Maryville announced the creation of the first corporate-named sport business management program in the nation. Williams says that putting the Rawlings name alongside Maryville allowed a spotlight to shine on the program like never before. It allowed students to concentrate their efforts in the areas where Rawlings needed help with their business—whether it was internships, research, projects, or serving as brand ambassadors in some way, shape, or form. The Rawlings partnership gave the program tremendous credibility and legitimacy within the sports industry.

Williams ranks that press conference alongside annual commencement ceremonies as the highlights of his Maryville career. His transition to academia has proven to be so natural that he currently serves as the assistant dean of the John E. Simon School of Business as well as the director of the Rawlings program. He also achieved tenure as a faculty member while earning his doctorate.

When Williams came to Maryville after almost sixteen years working in the sport business industry, he knew that if students were not given the all-important experiential experience, then the sport business program would not be successful. The program developed a philosophy where students learn the theory behind the topic of any particular course, but they also must "get their hands dirty" and put the theories they have learned in the classroom to the test in a real-world project. If you look at the St. Louis area during that time, there were then three major league sports teams, the St. Louis Sports Commission, the Missouri Valley Conference, Rawlings Sporting Goods, and other firms engaged in the industry in one way or another, Williams recalls. That environment was rich for student learning. Maryville acted quickly and took advantage for the benefit of its students.

Williams sought internship opportunities for his students by demonstrating that Maryville students could offer a great degree of value to firms. It sounds like a simple strategy, but he doggedly and continually asked those in the industry what types of skills they required of employees. Williams expressed a desire to partner with such firms to ensure that Maryville students were ready to provide value after they graduated and assume day-to-day responsibilities in the industry. "How can we best prepare these young people? And please tell us what we need to do to make them valuable to your organizations" is how Williams summarizes his outreach activities.

> **"How can we best prepare these young people? And please tell us what we need to do to make them valuable to your organizations" is how Williams summarizes his outreach activities.**

Williams has cultivated an avid core of program alumni who now help in providing opportunities for those students graduating from the program. Social media has allowed the program to make its network aware of employment opportunities that emerge around the world. It also allows the program's alumni to remain in close contact and network continuously. Those relationships do not end when students walk across the stage at commencement, grasp their diploma, and head to the exit, Williams emphasizes. Rather, they represent lifetime connections. His program's graduates know they can always come back to Maryville to receive assistance, advice, or encouragement.

ANOTHER ALUM SUCCESS STORY—DANIEL SCHMIDT

One of many examples of a student who has benefited from his experience in the program is Daniel Schmidt. Schmidt received his bachelor of science degree in 2010 in what is now the Rawlings Sport Business Management Program followed by his Maryville MBA in 2016. After he completed all his undergraduate academic requirements in the fall semester of 2009, Schmidt was immediately hired by the NHL's St. Louis Blues franchise where he had served as an intern. Schmidt worked for three years as program coordinator in the Blues corporate sponsorship department. Schmidt was seldom idle. He would juggle between twenty-eight to thirty-five clients each year. Some were small mom-and-pop operations. His largest was Anheuser-Busch.

Schmidt eventually transitioned to the Blues operations side, helping coordinate use of its Enterprise Center and its maintenance. Fourteen union personnel reported to Schmidt, which proved to be another valuable educational experience. Schmidt then extended his involvement beyond hockey. He helped advance a slew of concerts and shows that flowed through the Enterprise Center. The expertise he gleaned from this role, in fact, later qualified Schmidt to teach a facility management course offered within the Rawlings program. After five years with the Blues, he noticed that Maryville sought to hire a Rawlings program coordinator to concentrate primarily on career fairs, networking events, and communications outreach to broaden the name recognition and reach of the Rawlings program.

Since he had such a positive experience at Maryville as a student, Schmidt expressed interest in still being a dynamic part of its operations. He had come back to campus on occasion to speak to classes about his experiences with the Blues. Those interactions with students made him recognize and appreciate how much he truly loved Maryville and its surrounding community. He felt as if it was "kind of like going home" to accept the opportunity to work within the program. And his presence back at Maryville has helped cement a strong ongoing relationship with the Blues. Actually, several Maryville alums work in the Blues front office in a variety of roles.

Schmidt believes fervently that, in retrospect, his undergraduate experience that merged business acumen with experiential opportunities offered the perfect foundation for his notable career in the sports industry. He is pleased to be able to help other Maryville students find their own personalized path under the umbrella of the Simon Business School.

Williams contends that Maryville's culture of encouraging innovation and experimentation makes sense for all the people that the university educates—whether it be on campus, during a field trip to Texas or in an online class with students located anywhere in the world. He believes Maryville has taken a lot of traditional higher education philosophies and turned them upside down, in his view. Maryville has proved to be an institution that can do things differently with a different philosophy and be very, very successful.

AN EMPHASIS ON STUDENT NEEDS AT MARYVILLE

Campus refurbishment may best reflect Maryville's paramount emphasis on servicing student needs. Many institutions sprinkle the location of offices servicing students throughout campus. The reason is simple: the configuration of these offices reflects the configuration of the school's organization chart. The registrar's office reports to academic affairs, so it is situated there. Financial aid is often a function of admissions, so guess where that office is located? Student billing, the cashier, and other financial functions are usually located within the business office. Therefore, students are forced to tromp like nomads from hallway to hallway and sometimes building to building to locate the right place and individual who can help them.

Maryville resolved to turn that situation on its head. Student convenience became the paramount goal. The university created a Student Service Center (SSC) in 2008, incorporating financial aid, the registrar's office, the student accounting office, and the cashier in one location. No nomadic student treks were necessary anymore at Maryville after the Student Service Center debuted in 2008.

In 2017, the SSC morphed into the Division of Operational Excellence with a solution squad as its central element. Under Vice President Stephanie Elfrink, this group of fifteen professional staff operates across campus as a mobile unit, meeting students where they are, answering questions, and helping with billing, schedules, and all other issues utilizing the latest in mobile technology. In this way, Maryville operates more like an Apple store than a university, anticipating students' needs and creating one-stop flexibility in addressing most student questions and problems related to records, billing, financial aid, and such areas that traditionally are handled by a disparate group of administrative offices.

RENOVATIONS AND NEW BUILDING PROJECTS AT MARYVILLE

Recently, Maryville has engaged in a host of renovation and new building projects across campus. To achieve, Maryville is guided by three fundamental principles. The first principle employs a vision to create smart buildings, which are structures utilizing automated processes to control automatic functions such as heating, ventilation, air conditioning, lighting, security, and other systems. Such buildings together form an integrated smart campus where service and sustainability stand paramount. The second principle employs cutting-edge research in flexible modular design to allow learning and living spaces to be flexible, technologically sophisticated, and multipurpose. The third principle incorporates an abiding commitment that all of these spaces must serve the Active Learning Ecosystem first and foremost, because all spaces inside or outside throughout campus serve as learning spaces. While such facility work remains ongoing, the look and feel of Maryville continues to evolve, becoming less and less like a college campus of the 1960s and 1970s and more like a corporate headquarters of technology firms such as Google in Silicon Valley or Amazon in the Seattle area.

PHASE III

LEADING THE DIGITAL TRANSFORMATION AGE

Abraham Lincoln contended that the best way to predict the future is to create it.

Maryville's success provides lessons that form a blueprint for private and, indeed, all universities moving forward. These lessons are the foundation upon which higher education can seize the initiative, create a culture of continuous innovation, and ultimately shape the next great revolution of society—what some call the Digital Transformation Age or the Fourth Industrial Revolution (4IR).

LESSONS LEARNED

1. **Maryville University demonstrates the 80/20 rule: it spends 80 percent of its time looking out its front windshield and 20 percent glancing in its rearview mirror.** The heritage of rigorous academics inculcated by the Sisters of the Sacred Heart remains a bedrock principle of the university to the present day. This heritage is present both across campus in the historical markers and tributes to its past and also in its academic results with five nationally ranked academic programs, an 88 percent retention rate, and an

amazing 98 percent career placement rate. All are testimony to that heritage of excellence. Maryville, however, spends the bulk of its time looking out its institutional windshield to beyond the horizon. It expends great effort in learning about the latest trends in technology, curriculum, and the economic marketplace. It utilizes such learning to make informed decisions to position the university appropriately for its future. With a clear "over the horizon focus," Maryville anticipates the mega trends in education and society and is ready to meet its students where they are and not chase them from behind.

2. **Maryville remains relentlessly committed to sound, flexible planning.** Planning at Maryville is exemplified by intense focus rather than time allotted. Challenges, problems, and trends are studied thoroughly but rapidly by working groups designated to make specific recommendations to PAC within a firm timeline. In addition, key community members are constantly scanning the landscape for innovative tools and applications that can enhance and expand its unique brand of personalized learning. Central to this planning process is the commitment to implement its strategic plan from the board of trustees through institutional leadership to faculty and staff. One measure of successful planning and investment in the plan is that Maryville's first strategic plan running from 2007–2012 achieved 87 percent of its goals, and its current plan that runs from 2015–2022 has already achieved 75 percent of its goals, with eighteen months still to go. In short, planning at Maryville operates to ensure maximum success with institutional flexibility.

3. **Maryville focuses externally rather than internally.** The university has come to terms with today's fiercely competitive higher education marketplace. While positive examples from within the higher education industry are sometimes considered, the university is focused mainly on those successful disrupters of industry (i.e., Amazon, Google, and Apple Computers, among others) outside of education. This posture has led to Maryville forming enduring partnerships with businesses, governmental organizations, and nonprofits across a wide spectrum. These relationships help curriculum develop and evolve quickly while leading to the very best in student outcomes—including internships, problem-solving education, and, ultimately, career opportunities. Maryville's farsighted decision to create its Weekend & Evening College decades ago has allowed it to forge enduring ties to working adults, particularly in the twenty-five to fifty-five age range. This step set the stage for the university's partnership with Pearson to become a national leader in high-quality undergraduate and graduate online education. This approach means that a Maryville education is cutting-edge and dynamic while also leading to enrollment growth, ranking it as the second-fastest growing private university in the nation in 2020 according to *The Chronicle of Higher Education*.

4. **Maryville embraces new technology and techniques.** Initiatives such as the Digital World program in partnership with Apple have allowed faculty to shift pedagogy into a truly personalized approach to learning, creating what Maryville calls the Active Learning Ecosystem. With one of the top wired campuses in the United States, student learning can happen anywhere indoors or outdoors on campus. This platform allows

the mobile technologies of today to be facilitators of student learning and, of course, faculty engagement. From free iPads for all students featuring more than 150 learning apps loaded in to a fully digital course material platform for all students; to state-of-the-art faculty training where every faculty member receives two weeks additional salary to allow for two weeks of professional training workshops each May and August; to the current introduction of augmented, virtual, and mixed reality (AR, VR and MR) tools, Maryville is committed to educating students utilizing the expertise of tomorrow. To use an old cliché, Maryville "puts its money where its mouth is" concerning emerging technologies and techniques that put students first.

5. **Maryville acts this day.** Prime Minister Winston Churchill generated a continual stream of directives to British governmental agencies across the globe during World War II. The phrase "Action This Day" was stamped prominently in red letters on the first page of these directives to urge recipients to pursue speedy resolution. Maryville adopts Churchill's mindset across the university. Decisions are reached quickly. Issues do not fester. Uncertainty does not loom. At the same time, decisions are not made recklessly but prudently. They are integrated well with financial considerations. People are expected to work smart, effectively, and well together. And most importantly for the past staid culture of higher education, Maryville acts with a sense of urgency! Achievement and innovation are sought, rewarded, and celebrated. Failure in the process of innovation is not punished but rather turned into a learning moment to further accelerate achievement. Given the realities of the digital transformation

age and the corresponding pace of change, no one, certainly not universities, can afford any longer to move at a deliberate (some would say snail's) pace. Institutions now must make every day count through taking action and seizing the initiative.

6. **Maryville's disciplined financial practices form the bedrock of all other innovation.** For starters, Maryville has boosted enrollment significantly while diversifying its revenue streams and delivery mechanisms. Increasing numbers of traditional undergraduates, part-time students, and graduate students all contribute to university coffers. Next, careful thought has been paid to all physical campus enhancements to ensure that upgraded or new facilities satisfy student needs today and tomorrow. Additionally, the university has promoted instructional techniques that help keep costs low as well as introduce students to cutting-edge technology they will encounter in their working lives. Finally, the university's annual budgets and spending patterns are formulated and executed in an active, strategic way that reflect major institutional goals. Maryville's zero-based approach forces all strategic priorities to be funded properly and all other items not necessary to be reduced or removed from the process. This posture has led to substantial growth, allowing Maryville to freeze tuition and fees for four of the last five years from 2014–2019. It also will permit Maryville to lower its tuition by 20 percent over the next several years as part of its overall vision to create greater access and opportunity for all students regardless of socio-economic status. This process began during the 2020–2021 academic year when the university reduced tuition by 5 percent for traditional

undergraduate on-campus students. Maryville's press release outlining this move emphasized that "This tuition reduction is the next step in our phased approach to bend the cost curve back for families." Such action has been noticed and appreciated. One parent tweeted, "It's not every day you get a message from your child's college president telling you that tuition is being reduced by 5 percent this year and they have a goal to reduce it gradually by 20 percent! Way to go."

7. **Maryville satisfies its customers.** The university's customers—students/alumni and those who will employ them—demonstrate they receive a good return on their investment through professional success. The people who spend money on a Maryville education achieve excellent outcomes. They receive excellence, the highest level of instruction during their enrollment. That instruction translates into worthwhile and rewarding job opportunities afterward as demonstrated by its 98 percent rate for career placement after graduation. This simple formula translates into an excellent long-term return on their financial investment. Positive outcomes equal satisfied alumni. And satisfied customers are the best advocates that any university can possess. Maryville features them in abundance and demonstrates their success continually and in ways that are easy to comprehend.

8. **Maryville skillfully sequences its steps.** Maryville approaches its actions in the same way as a chess master: by carefully sequencing its steps. Nothing is left to chance. While unforeseen factors may require improvisation, the ultimate target remains visible. Many other institutions break down in the execution of their plans—most frequently by failing

to sequence their steps properly. In order to achieve strategic objectives, one must plan several moves ahead, anticipate issues, and make decisions in a sequence that enhances and, indeed, amplifies its positive results. For example, it may be a good thing to introduce four new academic programs and four new athletic programs, but the key element is in what order? Do them all at once, and you may not be able to invest in them sufficiently. Do the wrong one first, and you doom all others. But do them in the right order, and the success of one can actually amplify and enhance the success of subsequent programs. It is important for any institution to act with vigor and purpose. But all that effort may prove for naught if the institution has not acted *in the right way at the right time at the right intervals.* Maryville has sequenced its action steps effectively again and again. Most of life is timing. Master that requirement, and success often follows.

In 2014, Maryville proposed three new academic programs (two undergraduate and one graduate), two new sports, a new iPad initiative, and a new online nursing program.

The pressure to focus on new academic programs first was great because that's what universities usually do.

The iPad initiative drew some skepticism, as did online nursing. The two sports were considered as a last priority by most individuals. So what did Maryville do?

Maryville launched the iPad initiative, online nursing, and one of the sports programs, ESports, which had the greatest revenue/marketing/enrollment potential by far, first.

Result: Since 2015, enrollment has increased 68 percent while revenue increased 40 percent. Between the three new programs, the university garnered more than $10 million in earned (free) national marketing exposure. By launching those three initiatives first, sufficient revenues were generated to launch successfully all the other initiatives as well.

THE DIGITAL TRANSFORMATION AGE

We are now in the early stages of what scholars call the Fourth Industrial Revolution (4IR). This is commonly known as the Digital Transformation Age (DTA), although many analysts believe the pandemic has made it the Digital NOW Age. This dynamic fourth age is inexorably intertwined with the growth and evolution of technology. More specifically, accelerating digitization represents the convergence of technologies within the full spectrum of human life leading to profound cultural, socio-economic, and societal changes that not only impact people in all their actions and endeavors but fundamentally deconstruct, alter, and reconstitute business, education, healthcare, and social industries at their core level. This age is one of maximum and accelerating disruption. It would be almost a cliché to say that all of us, to varying degrees, are immersed in this new age and feel its disruption.

This digital reality is all around us, and it impacts myriad decisions and behaviors that people make each and every day. While mobile devices bring the world to us and project our personalized choices into that world, the fundamental assumptions on which socio-economic, political, and educational relations were based are being blown apart. This age is accelerating rapidly and brought into focus a critical second manifestation, which includes the emerging technologies of artificial intelligence (AI), augmented and virtual reality (AR and VR), and mixed reality (MR). These powerful tools are all powered by the limitless applications of data analytics. It is being felt in every industry to varying degrees and at different speeds. Perhaps the most visible and omnipresent examples are mega-entities such as Apple, Google, Amazon, Facebook, and Salesforce, among others. These businesses have harnessed the elements of this new age to disrupt and reshape huge aspects of the consumer society. In fact, they and others like them are in many ways leading this new age.

This digital reality has also shaken the very foundations of higher education and called into question its long-term viability both as a business model and a future model for education. Harvard Business School scholar, the late Clayton Christensen, studied and analyzed what he calls "disruptive innovation" in various industries, including higher education. This term underscores the incessant financial pressures that many colleges and universities face, regardless of the size of their endowments or the scope of public support. Christensen predicted that as many as half of the country's colleges and universities will find themselves bankrupt or shuttered within ten years. Many of these institutions will be small, private, generally rural institutions.

Whether Christensen's dire predictions prove accurate or not, statistical evidence indicates a steady and increasing percentage of colleges and universities that consolidate or close each academic year. The large majority (nearly 90 percent) of these shuttered institutions thus far are for-profit colleges. But the number of nonprofits closing has climbed since 2016. Many of these colleges have failed or merged due to one or more of the following circumstances: remote physical locations; dwelling on the past instead of properly planning for the future; obsolete curriculum and instructional techniques; slow institutional decision-making; declining enrollment; allowing deferred maintenance of the physical plant to become overwhelming; and lack of a clear strategic vision that positions the institution appropriately with prospective students and their families in the marketplace. All of these issues are clear signals that higher education has thus far failed to grasp the realities of this Digital Transformation Age.

Maryville, however, has embraced this new digital age and the values that undergird its evolution. Its foundational elements layered in over the past fifteen years have positioned it to harness these emerging tools to remake higher education. That foundation includes the following: It seizes innovative opportunities in programming. It has revolutionized the instructional pedagogy into an active learning ecosystem. Its curriculum is organic and evolving due to its extensive partnerships with professions and industry, including degree programs, certificates, and badges. Maryville has also remade the business model of higher education, skillfully carving out an identity as a nonexclusionary and affordable institution appropriate for a large segment of the population who seek intellectual challenge while developing demonstrable skills necessary to compete in a competitive global marketplace. And Maryville has recast the philosophy of student learning and service. As Dr. Lombardi has said countless times in speeches across the nation, "Everything inside the classroom should be challenging and stretch the intellectual capacity of students. But everything outside of it should be easy for the student with a service-first mentality provided by the institution."

What is next for Maryville as it harnesses the tools of this digital transformation age? In 2007, Maryville adopted a philosophy that betting on any "one thing" is fruitless and dangerous. Thus, its entire budgeting, personnel, and educational approach has been buttressed by the values of flexibility and mobility and showcases a unique ability among universities to pivot and take advantage of new opportunities and changing circumstances. It also has embraced a fundamental belief in the culture of innovation.

Vice Chair of the Board of Trustees Chris Chadwick, who chairs the Student Learning Outcomes Committee, notes that the university maintains a focus on where it wants to be in the future then works its way back from that vision to the present, concentrating particularly on the cultural changes needed to make such a transformation possible and successful. This is what Chadwick calls "right to left thinking." He argues that all disruptive leaders in their industry possess this quality. He emphasizes that while the university does move quickly and decisively, it does so by gathering information and understanding well ahead of future action, accompanied by keen anticipation. Chadwick points to the Pearson initiative for online education as an example of moving carefully at first with a piloted effort in graduate nursing. This approach and its success subsequently allowed the partnership to pick up steam and then sprint ahead. In five years, Maryville's online programs have grown from one to more than forty-five and from 350 students to nearly 8,000. Thus, spending extended time at first to carefully evaluate all considerations has allowed the university to move quickly later on.

Chadwick contends that the university focuses chiefly within academics on the type of education students will need in the future and associated revolutions in teaching pedagogy. This focus also includes a profound transformation of physical learning spaces that best facilitate personalized learning. The university will not seek to segment based on previous academic achievement or standardized test scores. It will not try to cull those who need additional time to adapt to higher standards of academic rigor or to find the right academic program for their requirements. It strives to allow each student to find their niche.

The university seeks to maintain flexibility and seize emerging opportunities. It particularly will continue to focus on investing wisely, building prudently, and managing costs to decrease its price tag and keep the cost of education affordable. Few academic institutions these days spend any time considering ways that they can lower their cost to create as much opportunity for as many of their students as possible.

Maryville, according to Chadwick and others, also recognizes the responsibility of universities like itself to strive to "close the loop" with K–12 education to ensure that students develop the type of skills they will need throughout all segments of their educational experience. That is a major reason why the university has cultivated close relationships with local school districts through its School of Education's Center for Access and Achievement (CA2). In 2019, Maryville initiated a program where its life coaching model would be embedded into selected school districts (such as Jennings and Riverview Gardens) and community partners (such as Boys Club and Girls Club of St. Louis) serving some nine hundred K–12 students from underrepresented groups across St. Louis. This approach is combined with a partnership initiative with major employers to prepare these and other students for emerging careers in fields such as cybersecurity, coding, data science, and more. This approach is ultimately designed to empower thousands of additional students with education and workforce skills that meet employer gaps and needs while elevating students, families, and communities who are often shut out of these economic opportunities.

The digital transformation age will only accelerate in the future. There are three main areas where Maryville leads the transformation of higher education: data lake, blockchain, and digital employees.

DATA LAKE

Like all businesses and universities, Maryville has utilized a variety of CRM (customer relationship management) tools designed to manage information and data. Most of these systems have a decidedly twentieth century perspective. In 2014, Maryville began a partnership with Salesforce to enhance the university's ability to interact with and understand its key audiences. This approach involved the consolidation of institutional research functions into a singular Office of Strategic Information (OSI), an expanded commitment to a transformational data analytics model, and the creation of what many now refer to as data lake. All of this activity was done to achieve the dual goals of data-driven decision-making and greatly enhanced student service, or as Maryville says, "Out-Amazon Amazon."

The data lake concept is simple. All universities collect data through multiple sources or systems. Converting all of that into one system like Salesforce is a laborious and long-term enterprise that can take years. By adopting Salesforce and driving future data collection through that CRM while also maintaining (where appropriate) legacy systems such as Colleague, Maryville creates a data lake from which OSI can draw data from multiple sources to analyze for decision-making and around-the-clock student service.

Many higher education institutions limit the use of Salesforce to specific areas rather than utilizing it across the board. But that is not the Maryville way. The university has tried to standardize its approach so that all departments throughout the university can partake and benefit. The university also acted to implement its use quickly, trying to fit an estimated four to six years of work into just two.

While Salesforce is a great platform, it is not a panacea for data or service issues. It is a tool to support an overarching paradigm that underscores the commitment of the Maryville community to make the life of their students better and simpler. This approach reflects the notion that higher education has transformed into a service industry where its "customers"—primarily students and others who pay tuition bills—expect the same customer experiences they enjoy in all other aspects of their daily life. To meet these student expectations, colleges and universities need to deliver on promises of streamlined, convenient services. And this goal has been much more easily accomplished institution-wide by aggregating and analyzing data through Salesforce and a broader data lake.

This new approach to data represents a significant cultural shift in higher education and the next generation of student service and data-driven decision-making across all divisions: academic, student life, enrollment, development, and finance. It also stands at the heart of reducing the cost of higher education to promote accessibility.

VICE PRESIDENT FOR STRATEGIC TRENDS—JEFFREY D. MILLER

Jeffrey D. Miller has had a long and impactful stint at Maryville. For most of his time at the university, he presided with success over the school's enrollment functions. Throughout this period, he worked in close partnership with Shani Lenore. In 2018, Mark Lombardi decided that it was time to promote Lenore to vice president of enrollment management. He also decided that the university needed a constant set of eyes and ears with respect to the cutting-edge trends, not just in education but in every other innovative endeavor. Lombardi created a new position within Maryville's hierarchy, the vice president for strategic trends, and tapped Miller for that role. His role is a novel one in the realm of academia and represents the futuristic culture of the Maryville mission and vision. And Miller fit the futuristic role perfectly.

For much of his tenure as president, Lombardi had devoted a significant portion of his own personal work time to studying emerging technological and societal trends. He had spent extended time examining all types of articles and information about topics as varied as artificial intelligence, virtual reality, blockchain technology, and digital employees. The time had come, he believed, to devote the energies of one person on a full-time basis to such endeavors. He knew Miller was the right person.

Miller is the first to admit his new position, while welcomed, was a bit of a sea change for him. His entire career had been devoted to being an implementer of policy. In his new role, implementation would not be a part of his portfolio. His charge, rather, would be to gather information and bring it back to campus to share. University leadership would then consider its ramifications and, where applicable, develop and execute implementation plans. Miller works largely from his laptop, traveling across the country to a plethora of artificial intelligence industry conferences and futurist think tanks while exemplifying the digital age at work. The governing principle of this exploration is simple: Maryville can learn the most, not from other universities, but from disruptive, cutting-edge industries and innovators.

Miller monitors scores of emerging trends at any given time. Most pertain to exponential growth or some type of disruptive technology. One current example is autonomous vehicles. Their effect will have a significant impact on physical campuses, parking lots, and student transportation systems—all of which could have a financial impact for schools and their students. While significant changes may still lie a few years down the road, the majority of the next generation of traditional college students might require very different transportation systems than their predecessors. Miller gathers such information and shares it on campus so others can begin to mull it over.

Miller monitors scores of emerging trends at any given time.

THE BLOCKCHAIN IMPACT

Another trend Miller studies is blockchain technology. Miller admits he knew almost nothing about this technology when he first assumed his position. He quickly learned that a blockchain is a digital public ledger that records online transactions. Cryptocurrencies, like bitcoin, utilize it as their core technology. Over time, its impact has become more pronounced elsewhere in everyday life. Miller points to Walmart using such technology in tracking its food supply. If, for example, an outbreak of contaminated lettuce would occur within the corporation's supply chain, Walmart can track it within seconds and know exactly which field the bad lettuce came from.

Blockchain technology has made some initial inroads into higher education. It has already changed the way a handful of institutions have begun to maintain and track records such as transcripts, diplomas, and credentials. When a student graduates, both their diploma and transcript can be placed in a "block" that only the student and university can access. The technique ranks among the most secure technology that is presently available in the market. Students could have ready access to their credentials in this way, something they have already earned and paid for. They can then instantly share such credentials via their cell phone with employers and others who need this verification, bypassing the cumbersome process of contacting the registrar's office at the school. Such technology provides a dual benefit: it allows the university to maintain efficient records needed for submission to governmental agencies and accrediting bodies while providing autonomy for students to access their transcripts and diplomas in a convenient way.

CHIEF DIGITAL TRANSFORMATION EVANGELIST— FENG HOU

One could argue that the most important discovery Miller uncovered during his travels was an individual by the name of Feng Hou. Miller heard Hou speak at several conferences regarding disruptive technologies. Hou served as chief information officer at Central New Mexico Community College (CNMCC) in Albuquerque at that time. Miller engaged with him in several conversations and a variety of interactions.

Miller decided to introduce Hou to Lombardi. After some conversations and an extended meeting at a Dallas airport described as informative and inspirational, Hou accepted an offer to serve as the university's chief digital transformation evangelist and began this function in June of 2019. Maryville intrigued him because the institution did not appear satisfied or complacent despite all it had achieved. Instead, it sought to push existing boundaries to continue to harness the power and potential of digital technologies. Hou's title is rare in academia but is actually commonplace in sectors of the corporate world—especially in Silicon Valley.

Hou's path to St. Louis proved circuitous. He grew up as the third child in a middle-class family in Wuhan, China, an industrialized city of millions of residents and the alleged place where some individuals believe COVID-19 first developed. Neither of his parents had attended college, although both of them prized education highly and encouraged their son's academic pursuits. Hou proudly notes that his father had joined a patriotic group that sought to thwart Japan's invasion of China during World War II, was wounded, and became a war hero. He notes—with some irony—that toward the end of his father's working career, he became involved in providing what today would be termed "professional development" or "continuing education" opportunities for workers despite his own lack of formal education.

Hou eventually became the first member of his family to earn a four-year bachelor's degree. He majored in American literature, consuming the words and works of authors such as Nathaniel Hawthorne, Edgar Allen Poe, and Mark Twain. After graduation, he was recruited to a local governmental agency that facilitated exchange programs between China and the West concerning science and technology. Eventually opportunities to travel abroad and serve as a translator or interpreter for government officials came his way. A retired businessman from Boston sponsored Hou to come to the US to further his education at Virginia Tech in computer science and education.

Hou spent several years teaching and working in the corporate sector as well as serving as CIO. Through his work experience, he became an expert in emerging technologies like blockchain and how universities and industry can reap the rewards of a digital transformation era.

During his stint as CIO at CNMCC, Hou instituted many new programs, but one initiative that garnered national and even international recognition pertained to a blockchain initiative. CNMCC became the first community college in the nation to implement a blockchain solution, thereby creating a student-owned learning credential solution that could be used with potential employers to verify their educational credentials. Instead of having to navigate the slow, costly, and cumbersome process of acquiring their transcripts, students could instead verify their credentials in a quick, free, and secure manner.

Hou notes that blockchain is ideal for this purpose because its security is immutable. Information cannot be altered or changed, hence the name "blockchain." It can only be amended. He contends it is simply a new generation of the internet that can carry value-based information instead of current data-based information. Thus, blockchain is an ideal solution for the record-keeping functions of a university to verify student credentials such as grade point averages, degrees earned, and training certificates completed. He sees long-term potential for institutions of higher learning to use blockchain technology to streamline and automate the verification of information for financial aid applicants as well as the credentials of lifelong learners—especially those who earned degrees at institutions that have since merged or become defunct. Blockchain offers a universal permanent record. As great as the technology is, however, Hou emphasizes that blockchain initiatives should never be done for the sake of blockchain itself. Instead, this technology will only prove successful if it supports a strategic initiative, such as allowing students a convenient and cost-efficient way to control the verification of their educational credentials.

This expertise in blockchain technology garnered Hou the chance to speak at many national conferences. His appearances at such venues first brought him to Miller's and, ultimately, Maryville's attention at a time when the university had determined it needed to hire an experienced and skilled digital professional who could spearhead the implementation of new technologies to develop more fully a data-driven, decision-making culture.

"With our unprecedented and continuous enrollment growth and our commitment to personalized learning for students, Maryville is positioned to fully use cutting-edge digital solutions for efficiency and scalability of processes, as well as utilize new and innovative digital tools to enhance learning," says President Mark Lombardi, PhD.

Hou believes one of his main gifts is the ability to be able to simplify technology for the benefit of the community, figuring out ways to reduce pain points. These are instances where individuals struggle to improve operations and promote efficiencies and benefit from removing barriers and/or obstacles. He refrains from pushing his viewpoints down the throats of others and avoids becoming an outlier. Instead, through meetings, dialogue, and conversations, he searches for ways to assist his colleagues in unison by opening their eyes to the possibilities that emerging technologies can bestow.

As one might imagine, the first goal the university has set for him is the implementation of a blockchain solution for learning credentials. His second designated goal is to assist in overhauling the university's academic program in computer science with a heavy focus in artificial intelligence and other disruptive technologies.

How does Hou define what he means by digital transformation at Maryville? First, whatever Maryville does, the end result must fundamentally transform the student experience. Second, it must improve operational efficiency through streamlining, optimizing, and/or automating existing processes. Third, it must dramatically reduce costs and promote greater access. A true digital transformation, in Hou's view, should accomplish all three goals—transform experience, improve efficiency, save costs—to prove worthwhile.

How does Hou intend to accomplish these goals? Again, he cites three factors. First, Maryville must continue to do the right things to ensure a top-notch experience for its students. But it cannot stop there, as many other institutions tend to do. Instead, it must also do things faster and more efficiently to free resources that can be deployed to clear other hurdles. Finally, it must scale progress in a way that can be extended throughout the university rather than quarantined to limited sectors.

Hou studies digital processes constantly. He reads at least one hundred pages each day to gather information. He admits to no bias in his sources, freely searching colleagues in academia as well as the corporate and governmental worlds in search of dynamic examples of digital transformation. He simply seeks to identify the truly leading sources of a technology and benefit from this expertise.

Hou has just begun to scratch the surface at Maryville. He has introduced a variety of initiatives for implementation including spatial computing, which incorporates virtual and augmented reality. Another is interactive storytelling, which emanates from gaming and could someday allow movies to offer various endings depending on the life experiences and inputs of a viewer. The latest trend he has discussed is something called complex event processing, which can process data in a much faster way to allow for quicker decision-making and dissemination of information in the case of, say, a campus emergency.

Hou hopes that one day Maryville may utilize such information to create a Center of Excellence for the Future of Work. He envisions it as a playground of sorts—whether physical or virtual—that further blurs the distinction between students and learners. According to Hou, digital transformation is a journey. It should not have an ultimate destination.

DIGITAL EMPLOYEES

Artificial intelligence is the primary focus of the Maryville digital transformation team made up of a small group of innovative faculty and staff that includes Miller and Hou. With industry partners, such as Capacity and Soul Machines among others, Maryville explores such concepts as deep learning and machine learning and their role in providing the foundation upon which all artificial intelligence is built.

Miller, for example, has devoted focus to the utilization of artificial intelligence through digital employees. These digital employees, who function like human avatars, have begun to be introduced by companies such as Mercedes-Benz to interact with and assist customers online. He envisions digital employees devoted 24/7 to servicing student needs. Such digital employees can be assigned a staff number, like human ones, so any interactions with students can be monitored and tracked back to that digital employee to ensure quality control. These digital employees, for example, can be utilized to replace or enhance the popular FAQs (frequently asked questions) section appearing on school websites. Maryville, in fact, introduced its first two digital employees, Mya and Emma, on its website in 2020, and three more will be added in the summer of 2021. In 2021, the first virtual digital professor in the United States will be launched. The digital sky has no limits.

Miller and Lombardi confer regularly to determine trends that should receive priority consideration. Ideas are vetted through the digital transformation work group. Pitches are then made to PAC regarding the best ideas. Thus far, all pitches have been slated and tracked for implementation, including initiatives such as digital IDs, certain certificates, and digital employees.

Miller estimates that of the myriad of conferences he has attended so far, only two have been sponsored by higher education entities. He operates largely as a lone wolf within his industry. Miller regularly keeps track of which institutions or organizations attend various conferences. Few university names appear. One think tank gathering last year featured only eight universities, the most he has witnessed. Many academic institutions, he has gleaned, try to monitor emerging trends, like Maryville, but do so in a less intense manner without someone occupying his full-time role.

Miller admits that he is sometimes perplexed when, after listening to a futurist, he questions the validity of their predictions and the worth of transmitting their concepts back on campus. But he finds there are just as many individuals whose knowledge is readily evident concerning topics such as the emerging 5G digital transformation and other topics.

CONCLUSION

The one thing many colleges can't do these days is stand pat.
The turbulent environment of higher education demands that
they distinguish themselves from their competition, make
plain their worth to their students and their communities,
and try to plan for the unpredictable decades ahead.

—"How to Make Strategic Big Bets,"
The Chronicle of Higher Education

Much is discussed and written these days about innovation and disruption in the world economy. No sector seems immune. That includes the traditionally staid higher education industry, which has arguably undergone greater transformation in the last decade than perhaps it did during the previous thousand years.

The future of higher education, like many industries, is fraught with peril. Many institutions are poorly positioned to deal with the revolutionary rigors of the digital transformation age. Maryville's story demonstrates there is a way to harness the tools of this emerging age and apply a new set of values and principles to create success while reshaping the future of higher education—thereby creating a new model for this century. Utilizing innovation, flexibility, speed, anticipation, prudent fiscal management, and a profound commitment to access and opportunity, Maryville has done just that. It will be intriguing, exciting, and perhaps even amazing to see what the university will create in the next decade and how many thousands of students— young and old—benefit from its disruptive and revolutionary spirit.

We've looked closely at why and how Maryville University crafted and implemented a strategy to remake many facets of higher education at a time when other institutions were stalled or pulling back in retreat. Why and how did this institution embed bedrock values—such as ambition, accessibility, speed, collaboration, courage, innovation, nimbleness, shrewdness, and vision—within its culture, causing it to act quickly and decisively? Why and how did this university update its delivery of services and forge a new model in personalized learning? Why and how has Maryville created a model for change in higher education that will light a path for its reinvention?

U.S. News & World Report has twice named Maryville the No. 1 Over-Performing University in the nation in 2013 and 2014 while *The Chronicle of Higher Education* designated Maryville as the second-fastest growing private university in the nation (2020).

This book is not simply a how-to volume for insiders such as college administrators, trustees, and faculty. This story, rather, is designed to provide a roadmap of a kind for varied readers—including students and their families. Designed to be a book that can be conveniently read during a cross-country airplane flight, it describes the traits of one institution that has navigated many hurdles by reinventing the values and principles on which universities have traditionally been based. These traits and examples of their application provide a framework for building the new university of the future—a university where no matter what the issue, student learning and outcomes remain paramount and always at the center. What may strike the reader is that the Maryville story is far afield from an institution utilizing a huge endowment or Nobel Prize-winning faculty of national prominence as springboards to success. Rather, this story demonstrates that it is precisely less heralded institutions like Maryville that possess a commitment toward freedom of action, flexibility of thought, and the courage to effect change. Many institutions pontificate about the need to effect change but back away when it comes time to act and implement. Maryville, instead, has forged ahead with courage, confidence, and resolve to lead a revolution.

ABOUT THE AUTHOR

Marty Parkes headed up the communications functions of Maryville University from 2009–2011. He also subsequently led the communications efforts for two private colleges located in Pennsylvania.

Parkes grew up as a Connecticut Yankee in the town of Ledyard, where he graduated from its public high school in 1977. He earned his BA degree in economics from Trinity College in Hartford in 1981. Parkes later completed a year of graduate study in international relations at The London School of Economics in England.

Parkes started his professional career in the corporate world working for two insurance companies in his native Connecticut. Then he gave up gainful employment to relocate and write about golf for the United States Golf Association. His service there spanned sixteen years, including the last eleven as its senior director of communications. Still, he remains an enthusiastic, if middling, golfer.

Parkes has published articles in varied publications such as *The New York Times*, *Golf Journal*, and *Sports Illustrated*. He authored the books *Classic Shots* (foreword by Arnold Palmer and afterword by Thomas L. Friedman) and *Up on the Hill* as well as contributed an essay to the book *Golf's Golden Age*.

Today he lives within walking distance of the nation's second oldest higher education institution, the College of William & Mary, in Williamsburg, Virginia. Parkes hopes such proximity to Thomas

Jefferson's alma mater has sharpened his intellect and enhanced this book.